A Psychological Handbook for Spiritual Directors

John J. Evoy, S.J.

Sheed & Ward

Sheed & Ward™ is a service of National Catholic Reporter
Publishing Company, Inc.

Library of Congress Catalog Card Number: 88-62584

ISBN: 1-55612-216-0

Published by: Sheed & Ward
                115 E. Armour Blvd. P.O. Box 419492
                Kansas City, MO 64141-6492

To order, call: (800) 333-7373

Contents

Author's Foreword

What prompted me to write this book? The increasing awareness that it was needed. This awareness arose from two different sources. One was my own accumulated experience from having given spiritual direction over the years. The other was what others had shared with me from their experiences as spiritual directors.

I am aware that since my professional background in psychology was known, a good number who came to me for spiritual guidance were also hurting psychologically. Other directors confided in me that conscientious people had looked to them for aid in spiritual growth and had not been helped.

The great majority of you who read this book will not be accomplished clinicians or psychological experts. Some of you undoubtedly will be. This book is directed particularly to those of you who are not.

What is the aim of this book? It is to help you, as a spiritual director, spot, in any one of those coming to you for spiritual direction, difficulties that are over and above the spiritual and moral ones. Then it is to give you some idea of what to do about these other difficulties.

How are you supposed to recognize the presence of the psychological? This would be primarily the case in situations where you might have suspicions that something more than just the spiritual and/or moral could be present and yet not be sure. I know of no simple, neat way to make you sure. I hope nonetheless, by means of this volume, to increase your confidence that when you *sense* deeply the presence of a psychological difficulty you will trust that response.

What is the difference between psychological counseling and spiritual direction? To dwell on this distinction at length would take us afield of our subject matter. Yet this distinction does indeed warrant some attention, because of the difference between theory and practice.

In theory while both psychological counseling and spiritual direction attempt to help people, they have a very different *goal*. Psychological counseling endeavors to help people increase their psychological health. Spiritual direction seeks to aid people understand the workings of the Holy Spirit within them. That's the theory.

The practice does not always correspond to this nice clean division. It may run the gamut. Most people in spiritual direction are well balanced, even though many of them, not unlike ourselves, have their little idiosyncrasies and problems. Then there are others. What are you likely to encounter in some of these others? For instance, a person who has been advised to get professional help for emotional behavior problems may feel that going to a 'shrink' is either too expensive or else shameful. So he quietly compromises by going to someone "for spiritual direction." Still others, irrespective of their understanding, show up for spiritual direction burdened with serious feeling-emotional conflicts. Even if you have been professionally trained to help such people would you want to do it *as* a spiritual director?

Ought you as a spiritual director nevertheless hope to be able to benefit some of these hurting ones? My judgment is that you should. To begin with, the true, primary SPIRITUAL DIRECTOR of every one who comes to you for such help is none other than the Holy Spirit. You, as *spiritual director*, on the other hand, need only try to assist. In no sense, then, do you assume the primary responsibility for guiding a person through life's trials and dangers. Moreover, you are not without the ongoing help of the Holy Spirit in doing your part. You may also judge, that you should continue spiritual direction with a person *only* when that individual is receiving profession psychological help, as well.

You would, I think, wisely remind yourself occasionally that in coming to another for spiritual direction a person does not thereby surrender all his(her) rights to personal privacy. I have favored a policy of *rarely probe* in any sensitive, delicate, personal area.

Adhering to this *rarely probe* policy has not always been easy. I have at times judged that I lacked sufficient (delicate) information to help a person. My own finding is that once these people discover by experience that they are free to talk about delicate matters and drop them at any point, they then enjoy the liberty of returning to them later if they think they are important. And normally, I have found they do return to them, usually several times, revealing one aspect at a time.

I have often found that a person needs to know for sure that he(she) can talk about anything without fear of being placed "in the dock" by his well-meaning director. *Trust* is a very large factor in one's relationship to you, his spiritual director, and he needs to feel his way in thus coming to trust you.

In a number of the examples given in this book I suggest that you refer individuals for professional help. Coming to you for direction will be some who manifest feeling-emotional problems you judge call for professional help. Should one of these people suggest receiving such help from a spiritual healing ministry, what ought you to do? My own position is this. I would be very loathe to discourage such an undertaking unless I had reasons to be distrustful of the minister indicated. I have no doubt whatever that God *can* heal such a person in this way. Whether He *will* is another matter, one which I feel is ordinarily not mine to judge. The exception, as I indicated, would occur if I had grounds for thinking that the contemplated healer was highly untrustworthy. What about your referring someone to a professionally trained person, such as a psychiatrist, psychologist or trained social worker? After many years I have come to a somewhat surprising position. I have a strong disinclination to refer a practicing Catholic to any professional person who is not himself or herself a practicing Catholic. This is not to assume that every clinician who is a practicing Catholic is thereby a good clinician. That has to be judged in each case.

Why only to another practicing Catholic? Because the passing of years, education and prayerful reflection bring to one who is living this faith the increasing realization that the whole meaning of life and basic life-values come from his(her) faith. One who does not live that faith, even if giving respectful recognition to its tenets, does not share these momentous life areas with this person. Nor does such a one comprehend their reality for living as does the person who tries to live them. Hence, while the psychological help given such a person by a competent clinician who does not live this faith, can be very helpful, it will be limited to relatively surface help.

How would I suggest that a practicing Catholic evaluate the professional competency of a clinician who is a practicing Catholic? Ultimately, I think, it is a personal evaluation. Tell the person you are referring, "See whether you can really begin to talk, without excessive discomfort, to this professional person. Observe whether you start to feel that you might be able to trust him(her)."

My own experience has been that the right professional individual often is simply not available especially in the smaller towns. And even were such an individual accessible, someone might feel that he(she) could not afford the publicity that would be inevitable in regularly seeing this professional.

Is there, then, nothing such a one could do to get help? In such a situation I tell the person something that some clinicians perhaps would not agree with. I suggest, "Look to see whether you might find someone in your area whom you feel you could begin to talk to and trust. The trust would mean that you would feel this person could keep a confidence and also not think less of you no matter what you might say. Then say to this person, 'Could I just talk with you for an hour once a week? Your role would be *just to listen* and *try to understand* what I will be endeavoring to say. That's all. No advice or encouragement or any other response will be needed or expected. On my part, I will have no idea of how to proceed, where to start, how or where to go. Yet on something like a blind act of natural faith, I believe, because I was told, that after a time this will begin to help me deal with my feelings and emotions.'" (In what follows, I refer to the person playing the role of listener as the TRUSTED LISTENER.)

"You might even want to explain to this TRUSTED LISTENER the basis for all this. Tell him(her), "Psychologically it has been found that when a person has an opportunity to show his(her) problem to another person who *tries* to understand, he sees it more clearly himself and so can begin to deal effectively with it." You might remind the one you are advising, "If you really *need* another human being, God will make that person available. Why? Because He loves you." Finally, note that this TRUSTED LISTENER procedure does not appear capable of producing notable therapy with every psychological difficulty. It should give help with some, however. The expectation is that for unmistakable help it could take many weeks. The anticipation is that it will do no damage to those it does not help. Still it would be wise to discontinue it should the one talking begin to discuss suicide, the killing of another, or some other most uncomfortable problem.

We have just considered the person who cannot or may not be referred for professional help. What of the one you sense ought to be referred for such help? How do you go about it? This is a most significant question because referral *can be* a devastating experience. A person being referred can feel, "I finally got the courage to dare show my real self to another and what did I get? One glimpse of the utterly disgusting real me and he(she) couldn't wait to get rid of me. That's all I needed!" How do you avoid giving such hurts? I would suggest telling the person something like this. "Since I have not been professionally trained in the feeling-emotional aspects of spiritual direction, would you consider also seeing one who is professionally trained in these feeling-emotional aspects? Unless you already have someone in mind, I have heard some good things about one person. It might be worth checking to see if he(she) could help you in these areas, while we deal with your spiritual life."

Ought you *also* to be a clinician or a TRUSTED LISTENER for one coming to you for spiritual direction? Generally speaking, I would think this unwise, unless you are a professionally trained clinician. And you must be ready to guard yourself against being pressured into playing a clinical role by a very anxious, even desperate pleader. I would suggest that in such a situation you continue with him(her) in spiritual direction, if you think you should. Meanwhile, as far as possible, sidestep all this person's feeling-emotional problems. At times that is by no means easy to do. I think that as you read through this book, you will find some helps to accomplish this.

Why do people seek spiritual direction? Any one answer would be simplistic. Many feel that it will help them grow spiritually. Some recognized U.S. pacesetters in spirituality maintain that having a spiritual director is a *must*. Other people have been moved to it by a notable experience in a directed retreat, cursillo, marriage encounter, shared prayer experience, or such. There are those who feel that to be able occasionally to discuss their spiritual life with a knowledgeable, understanding person is beneficial. Occasionally, and I think unfortunately, a person goes for spiritual direction solely because this person feels he(she) has no other choice.

For instance, I recall one woman who did not seem to be making much progress in her spiritual direction. She struck me as a good person and this baffled me. After a period of time she said, "It wasn't my idea." Then she explained that she experienced revulsion at the prospect of having to open up her personal life to some other person. Going for spiritual direction had become the *in* thing in her group of friends. "When someone asks me," she added, "Who is your spiritual director?" I want to answer, "None of your damned business." In this case the pressure presumably was coming from persons who wanted the best for her. Yet that pressure, for her, approximated personal violation. I told her that this must be her choice if she was to benefit from spiritual direction. I suggested that after prayer if she preferred to come to me for a short visit every two weeks or so, so she could truthfully say she went to a spiritual director, that would be acceptable to me. Within less than a month she returned and said she would like to try spiritual direction. She continued in it and showed clear signs of spiritual growth.

On occasion I have talked with men who prefer a woman spiritual director. It is just their preference. A couple have explained, "I like to get a woman's viewpoint." I have encountered some women each of whom has said she feels the need, at times, to talk to a man rather than to another woman about her personal life. This man needs to be someone who will listen and understand. The reasons I have most frequently been given are: 1) She finds that somehow this helps her see some things more clearly and objectively; 2) "I don't trust women." Occasionally a person comes to a spiritual director simply because he(she) is lonely and most eager to talk to someone. And this spiritual director is available. These persons are usually not difficult to recognize. They are not interested in discussing their spiritual life. They have come to visit. Once recognized, you are in a position to reflect, "Do I want to visit with this lonely person? If not, shall I tell this person I do not feel comfortable with this relationship and would prefer he(she) go to someone else?"

Something that on the surface looks a bit like the last mentioned lonely person approach comes from something utterly different. It is the bewildering behavior of the person who initially is not really telling you anything, yet, you feel, is just having a great deal of trouble getting started. It can well be that the person is feeling you out to see, "Can I really confide in you?" Should you pass the testing period, this person's story may come rolling out with signs of tremendous relief.

Lastly some mention should be made of the person who, over a period of time, makes it increasingly clear that he(she) is developing an over-admiring, romantic relationship with you. Everything you say is being interpreted by this person in a sentimental, interpersonal context. Through a fantasied perception your every word and gesture are being viewed as unequivocally fanciful. When this person finds it impossible to win your open affection, look for an excessive striving for your exclusive attention.

How is such a person to be dealt with? I know of only one way. I do not see that this falsified perception can be corrected. Before this person can be given the chance to make any spiritual progress you must free him(her) from the obsession with you. How? As gently as possible tell him that ACCORDING TO YOUR CONSCIENCE you are not the one to be his(her) spiritual director. Explain that it is to be a complete break, with no phone calls and no written word. That's it. Above all, do not argue about it with this person. Since you are following your conscience, it is to be understood that this is how you feel about it, rather than giving your reasons for it.

This book is meant to help you become more aware of the psychological, over and above the moral and spiritual, aspects of a given personal problem. I have not attempted to do this by theoretical explanations. Instead I have fleshed out actual instances of such psychological contents taken from my own experiences in giving spiritual direction over the years. Needless to say these have been presented in such a way that the identity of those involved is concealed from everyone but these persons themselves.

In addition, I hope to increase your understanding of the *meaning* beneath these reported experiences and/or behaviors. This I have endeavored to do by presenting the UNDERLYING MEANING of each. Lastly I have offered you some SUGGESTIONS ON WHAT TO DO when confronted with the person reporting one or more of these experiences and/or behaviors.

Now a few practical considerations relevant to your spiritual directing. As a spiritual director you cannot, in my judgment, be too considerate, or too gentle. You can, however, be too kind. Kindness is not synonymous with love. At times to be kind is to be hurtful. So this would not be love. You may be begged to make someone's personal decisions, or be pressed to permit someone to structure an unhealthy dependency on you. I think you would wisely foresee the approach of an agonizing person imploring you, "If you love me or really care about me, you will do such and such." At times it is extremely difficult to go counter to such a plea. Yet you need to decide for yourself how you will express your concern for each individual.

Then there is the matter of time. How much time ought you to allow for each person in a given spiritual direction session? It seems apt here to look at spiritual direction both within a directed retreat and outside the time of retreat.

During a directed retreat usually you will have several people to see every day. Normally these persons are scheduled for about 30 minutes each, daily. In my experience, this appears to satisfy the majority of retreatants. Yet, I anticipate that there will be at least one who needs to talk over something which simply cannot be scheduled within a prearranged time slot. So, on the first day I tell each one I'm directing, that if more time should be needed, to just let me know. I schedule conferences either in the morning or afternoon. The other half of the day the person may come for as long as he or she wants. It usually takes a few days before one of these persons feels it is safe really to talk to me.

How much time ought to be given to individual conferences outside the times of retreat? Most persons, in my experience, seem to require anywhere from about half an hour to an hour. Very seldom do they vary greatly on the time each takes. In general, I have found, men take less time. Many of them have a way of summarizing what they see as their relevant experiences. I have observed that many women have found everyday happenings with their individual characteristics and details very important in their assessment of their spiritual progress. The remarkable Caryll Houselander seems to present their view of it in her book, *The Reed of God,* when she says, "Yet it is really through ordinary human life and the things of every hour of every day that union with God comes about." Many women have seemed able to appreciate this and operate off it as a base.

In my experience a very few people require about two hours each session. They choose to proceed on the basis of what appears to be a blow-by-blow account especially of their recent life happenings. Some of these have said that they are thus letting the spiritual director get to know them. So important is this approach to a few of them that they find it exceedingly difficult to go to a new director in a directed retreat, who "doesn't know me."

What is to be said of a not uncommonly overheard remark such as, "Every properly prepared spiritual director should have some familiarity with the theoretical contributions of such psychological giants as Freud, Adler, Jung, Fromm, Horney, Sullivan, Maslow, Skinner, Rogers, Binswanger, etc."? I am not in favor of this position. Given the lack of agreement among these experts, such a familiarity could be confusing and even hurtful to you. In addition it might quite unconsciously influence you to move into the role of psychological counselor. After better than 30 years experience as a psychological counselor I am familiar with the problems confronting the psychological counselor endeavoring to confine himself to the proper role of a spiritual director.

Finally, I recommend:

a) that you read right through the book to get the overall picture.

- It will reveal what else besides moral and spiritual considerations can underlie personal difficulties.

- It will indicate when, why and how a person ought to be referred for professional help.

- Some of your own convictions and/or practices in the area of spiritual direction will be confirmed.

- You will be more alert in recognizing what is and is not properly within your role as spiritual director.

b) that you retain the book as a useful handbook for ready reference. The alphabetical arrangement of the examples will usually make it easy to find an experience and/or behavior similar to the one confronting you at any given time.

- Hopefully you will remember that, when in doubt, just listen.

1. Achievement

Difficulties Presented: [younger, middle-aged priest] This man with a graduate degree had been teaching in a university. Aware that God endowed him with a fine mind, his problem, he said, was that he was experiencing no peace in his teaching position. It was becoming an agony that he was not receiving the recognition and acclaim that could be available to him in a much larger university. "There I could be a big fish in a big pond," he explained. "Yet what if that university proved to be too big and I found I was just one more of the big fish? Would I not do better to come back to the small pond where I would really be somebody outstanding?"

Underlying Meaning: This man quite unwittingly was revealing an almost obsessive drive to prove his personal adequacy by recognized achievement. Unfortunately this feeling of personal inadequacy, which dates from his early life, isn't disproven that way. One can never prove his personal worth or value, i.e., what he *is* by what he *does*. Accumulative recognized accomplishments never translate into felt, personal adequacy. Still, for him, it is unthinkable that he would settle for his current low self-concept and he knows no other way to try to cope. The regrettable but predictable fact is that no matter how much recognized achievement he experiences he will continue to be tortured by this feeling of being inadequate.

Suggestions On What To Do: This kind of person could benefit from the right professional help. Whether and when to suggest this to him(her) calls for the wisdom of Solomon. What grounds could you give him for wanting to refer him? At the same time it would be most unlikely that spiritual direction, by itself, might notably help him. He would be far too preoccupied with the need of showing people his achievements to be consistently concerned about spiritual progress. Because he is intelligent, there is always the hope that on his own, with grace, he will come to recognize his need for professional help. Thus he becomes an apt subject for prayers.

2. Addiction

Difficulties Presented: [younger, middle-aged married woman] Although this woman had a number of emotional problems she was genuinely concerned about her spiritual growth. She had been careful to take only the drugs her physicians had prescribed and only in the doses prescribed. Yet, she finally had to admit to herself that she was completely addicted to drugs. When she told two of her doctors about it, she said, they both looked at her and sort of shrugged, without even suggesting what she might do to free herself from these addictions. In order to relate to God as she thought He wanted her to, she felt she needed to be freed from the enslavement to these drugs.

Underlying Meaning: Clearly a person can become badly addicted in this way. Usually there are other personal problems, as well, for which the drugs have been prescribed. But to progress spiritually the person does need to be freed from these addictions, and unfortunately the rate of success is not at all high in achieving such freeing on any lasting basis. It is the tremendously strong interdependence of the spiritual on the psychological and bodily health which makes the freeing imperative.

Suggestions On What To Do: As spiritual director you would, of course, have no part in dealing directly with the addictions. But your support and encouragement would be very reassuring to such a person looking for escape from these addictions. As you continue your spiritual direction with her(him) you might also be able to refer her for other professional help. At the same time it would be well for you to pray for and with her.

3. Addiction

Difficulties Presented: [young woman religious] In her nursing career she found herself seriously overworked with no practical way of reducing her work load. She experimented with one of the drugs as a 'pick me up'. On the verge of exhaustion, she received surprising energy from it. She repeated and before long found herself addicted to it. Eventually she had to go away for special treatments. This was with the knowledge, in strict confidence, of only her superior. When she returned, cured, she was aghast to find that others in the community knew of 'her problem'. In talking to her of her employment possibilities they let her know clearly that she could not be given any position that carried responsibility for the keys to any drug drawer. Those who had treated her medically were enthused at her remarkable recovery. Not so, however, her community. In their eyes she still had 'her problem', and was never let forget it. Repeatedly she was terribly hurt by them.

Underlying Meaning: The mistrust and disbelief of one's own religious family can be excruciating. Because this woman had failed at one time, they would not let her up. When she told them of her remarkable recovery, they politely declined to believe her, which she said almost killed her.

Suggestions On What To Do: Once such a person feels you really know her(him) you can give her great moral support. When she sees that you are compassionate and that you trust and believe her, Jesus becomes for her more real and credible. This support, despite the pain coming from her fellow religious, can enable her to benefit considerably from spiritual direction.

4. Addiction

Difficulties Presented: [middle-aged, single man] During a retreat this man said that he had a number of weaknesses by reason of which he repeated week after week the same sins. He had been convinced for a long time that the key to his overcoming them would be to give up smoking cigarettes. For him, control of his smoking somehow represents his being able to control his life. He had tried repeatedly to quit without real success. Badly discouraged, he said he had talked to a confessor about this and had been told that if he had enough faith and loved God enough he would be able to discontinue smoking. Then he said, "I prayed and I tried but I haven't broken from the cigs. I always thought that I believed in God and wanted, despite my frequent failures, to lead my life the way He wanted me to. Now I wonder if I have any faith or love for God. It sure doesn't look like it. I'm considering tossing in the towel. I suspect that God has given up on me anyway; so, what's the point of trying?"

Underlying Meaning: I have learned to pay attention to the hunches of people who are struggling emotionally. This man's hunch that his control of smoking somehow stood for his overall self-control was most likely very significant in conveying to him what was really going on within him. One result of what he understood the confessor to say was hurtful and destructive rather than helpful. I did not find out what was beneath all these experiences, though I would sense definitely it was considerable.

Suggestions On What To Do: From this example, among others, note the danger in trying to place a spiritual poultice on a psychologically-based festering sore. The last state of the man was worse than the first. (One wonders how many have tossed in the towel or otherwise been hurt, because of some well-meant spiritual advice! On the other side of the coin, one wonders how much harm has been done by well-meaning guides who sought to deal with every personal difficulty solely by psychological means!) When you see someone for only a very short time, as during a retreat, there may be very little, in addition to listening, you can do that will be really beneficial to the person. Given sufficient time you could refer him(her) to the right professional help with this problem of self-control, while you continue to give him spiritual direction. Should the right professional help not be available, a TRUSTED LISTENER relationship (cf. Author's Foreword) might prove helpful.

5. Affection Hunger

Difficulties Presented: [middle-aged, single woman] This woman said she longs to be held affectionately not as a woman would be held by a man but as a little child would be held by an adult. She doesn't really expect anyone to understand this almost consuming hunger to be held warmly and affectionately on the lap of a loving woman or man. Yet this yearning has been with her as long as she can remember, and it drives her constantly. She added that all her adult life she has been searching for such a person. And she knows that she is doomed to inevitable frustration, because if she ever found such a person, since she is an adult she could never permit herself to be thus held as a child.

Underlying Meaning: Unfulfilled basic needs in early childhood do not just go away nor do they gradually fade. Instead such needs remain along with their original age characteristics. That is why I was not surprised when this woman volunteered that she could not remember as a child ever having received affection from her mother or father. It should be noted that this kind of psychological aftermath admits of a large span of degrees. It ranges from the adult who is still psychologically in almost every way a child, out to the otherwise psychologically mature person, who happens to have a persisting child-hunger for a particular form of affection.

Suggestions On What To Do: When and even whether you ought to explain to such a person why her(his) unsatisfied childhood hunger maintains itself with its childish characteristics, you would wisely decide only after you have listened for some time. Some persons with this problem have been helped by being shown that this is their peculiar cross, which God will give them the strength to carry. You might tell such a person that God *could* if He wishes, remove this cross. And she is free to ask God for this as long as she leaves Him free to love her as He wants. If you begin to see that you are confronted with a child in a woman's or man's body you will not be able to accomplish much with spiritual direction alone. You would wisely endeavor also to refer her for professional assistance, perhaps telling her that you do not feel qualified to help her with these inclinations and feelings.

6. Affection

Presenting Difficulty: [young single man] This is a religious seminarian. He remarked that he greatly fears he will be assigned to a house which has a large number of religious. As he explains it, any religious house resembling an institution simply cannot provide for his affective and social needs. He craves the intimate companionship of a few who live together, pray together, work together, recreate together and care deeply for one another. Otherwise, he said, he is not nurtured. If he is not nurtured, he knows he will shrivel up as a person. Because he has serious misgivings about establishing such personal relationships outside his community, he feels an unmistakable need for them in community.

Underlying Meaning: The emphasis on small-group living in religious communities is a relatively recent phenomenon. Nonetheless in previous times some religious, at least, were aware of their need for real friendships. Some even felt that a large house of men or of women offered greater opportunities to choose and pick one's close friends. The awareness of one's needs for friendship in one's living situation appears to be healthy. There is something in the case of this young man that raises some questions. It is what appears to be approaching the community as though bringing a couple of empty affection buckets to be filled by the warm, tender feelings of others of the community. If one's primary motive for entering a marriage were, "This person can fill all my needs," there would be real grounds for concern. That's not a giving orientation; it's a getting one! In regards to this particular religious, we wonder if we are encountering an 'affection hunter.' Such a person can be a one-person plague in a religious community.

Suggestions On What To Do: Your sensitive listening coupled with the delicate seeking of clarification regarding wholesomeness of motivation might prove very helpful. This is clearly an area where, after prayer, you will need to trust the correctness of your own 'vibes,' since probably you can't be sure. You might even become convinced that you would have to raise the vocational question whether a religious so engrossed in fulfilling his(her) own needs, gives real promise of being able to commit his life to fulfilling Christ's goals.

7. Affection

Difficulties Presented: [young, single woman] She maintains that she must fight against God, especially against accepting and returning His love. In her eyes affection is a dangerous weakness. Her father, she says, was very affectionate, loving, lovable and yet an almost unbelievably weak milk toast of a man. Her mother was a woman of amazing strength, something of a human pillar of the family. Her mother's love was principally a love of the mind rather than of the heart. It recognized accomplishments and strengths. Now this young woman sees joy and peace in those who are openly warm and affectionate, but she also shudders at their terrible vulnerability. Her main concern with herself is that she is not more productive.

Underlying Meaning: This kind of person subscribes to the position that man is a wolf to his fellow man. To give and especially to accept affection is to expose oneself to attack, assault, being wounded, used, and walked over. In order to accept any expression of love from any person she must see it as something else, e.g., appreciation, duty, kindness, something earned, etc. She cannot even begin to let God love her. She cannot accept His love as such. What, then, is her source of personal worth and value? It is recognized achievement, which was her mother's norm. She *has* to try to prove her personal worth over and over. This is all in vain. She is not a free woman.

Suggestions On What To Do: You cannot be too gentle with such a person. You might ask her(him) to pray over Francis Thompson's *Hound of Heaven.* If she persists for several months in fighting the acceptance of God's love and/or all human love, you could explain to her that she has come to her present position honestly, but unfortunately it is not a healthy position spiritually or psychologically. Tell her that while she is seeing you, you would also like her to have professional help with this problem, if such is available.

8. Aggression

Difficulties Presented: [younger, religious priest] This troubled man had been teaching at a Catholic college. He felt that his superior had unjustly removed him from an upper division class in which he was lecturing on his specialty, to a high school where he is presently teaching little kids what he calls 'mickey-mouse' courses. "I resent every minute I have to spend with those little brats, he remarked, but I'll never let them know that. What annoys me is that some of them told another faculty member that I didn't like them. And believe me, I've never let on, though I suppose that some of the penalties I've given them have perhaps been a bit heavy."

Underlying Meaning: This religious appears to be smarting under the humiliation, frustration, hurt and anger from the 'unjust' demotion. There is no way such a person may express anger directly toward his superior, because of the commitment to obedience and the other one's position of authority. What this man does not clearly recognize is that he is taking it out on the kids. Psychologically it amounts to trying to get even, and since he is not really aware of the injustice of what he is doing, he doesn't have to square it with his conscience.

Suggestions On What To Do: Well aware that this type of person is showing insecurity, you need to feel your way most delicately in what counsel you offer. Obviously to confront such a one directly with the fact that he(she) is employing aggressive behaviors against these youngsters, could be highly threatening to him. To try to appreciate his hurt and his spontaneous tendency to hurt back safely, however, might give you the opportunity of gently suggesting that this might be a displacement of the urge to hurt back. If he is able to own his displaced aggression, he will probably be capable of acknowledging his own hurt in its depth, and begin consciously to cope with it. If, on the other hand, he balks at the slightest approach to the idea of displacement, he is telling you that this area is untouchable. As such, without professional help, he does not give much promise of spiritual growth. Unfortunately any attempt to refer him for professional assistance would very probably be futile. If you choose to continue as this person's spiritual director, you'll need great patience. Under the circumstances, with a TRUSTED LISTENER he might in time recognize the displacement of his hostility, and from there receive further insights into some of the dynamics operating below the level of his awareness. If and when he came to view these as the dynamics that had been motivating him, he would be moving toward greater psychological and spiritual health.

9. Alcoholic Problems

Difficulties Presented: [middle-aged, married man] This man came during a directed retreat. He said that he had just been terminated in his position because of what his business superiors chose to term his "Drinking problem." He said they were overreacting to the problem. He had missed a few days in the office and come late several times. But he explained that it was not that big a thing, even though it had cost him two previous jobs. To make it worse, his wife was also overreacting. She was seriously talking about separation. He said he would concede there was *some* difficulty there. In fact, that is why he had come on this retreat. He needs God's help and not the Alcoholics Anonymous stuff they have been 'bugging' him with. He said that he feels certain that if God does not cure him during this retreat, then spiritual direction will enable him to straighten out this area and the rest of his faults.

Underlying Meaning: Regardless of how his problem would be explained, unhealthy thought patterns are manifest. The assumption is that there is a good deal wrong psychologically in this man. His drinking, among other things, is a REACTION to some of these deep psychological needs. Drinking is a way, though an unhealthy way, of dealing with these needs. To this can be added the probability that this man simply is unable to handle alcohol.

Suggestions On What To Do: In no way would you encourage him to expect God to cure him of his problem during the retreat. Neither would you concur with his anticipation that spiritual direction is the route to the solution of his problem. He is not going to be able to pull this off all by himself. He needs help. You could tell him that he could look for relief from his problem by combining spiritual direction with the A.A. program or professional help. By no means should he think solely of the spiritual direction and dismiss the other.

10. Aloneness

Difficulties Presented: [middle-aged, single man] This man remarked, "I can't stand the aloneness. There is no one in the entire world I value, who really cares whether I live or die." He summed it up with the statement, "Not one of the important people in my world has ever loved or cared personally about me."

Underlying Meaning: I like to distinguish *loneliness* (lonesomeness) from *aloneness* The first, *loneliness,* is a warm pain. It is warm because it bespeaks the existence of someone whose love the person values and wants and who loves that person. It may also be distressing because geographical or temporal absence from such a one is invariably deeply painful. The man here is describing not *loneliness* (lonesomeness), but rather *aloneness.* This latter is the feeling that there is no other person whose love he wants who loves him. This is a devastating experience. Regardless of terminology, the two experiences are as different as day and night. A person experiencing *aloneness* is psychologically wounded.

Suggestions On What To Do: You should recognize immediately that such a person is in need of a professional clinician. Real spiritual growth in such a circumstance while not impossible would be most unlikely. Accordingly, you might tell this person you would be glad to be his spiritual director if he also gets professional clinical aid for these feelings of aloneness. Tell him he will need assistance to cope successfully with these, and you do not feel qualified to give this kind of help. Should professional help, for whatever reason, not be possible for him what could you do? You might suggest to him that he look about for a TRUSTED LISTENER (cf. Author's Foreword). Such a person might conceivably come to be one whom he cares about and who cares about him. Should this process begin, it is hoped that the other person would expect to be tested again and again by the one suffering from aloneness. Such a hurting one just cannot believe that someone of worth really cares about him(her), and is not just pretending to do so.

11. Aloneness

Difficulties Presented: [middle-aged, single woman] This woman reported that she experiences loneliness, hurt and guilt. She mentioned that she has many longings. Her keenest hunger she characterized as an almost consuming yearning to be *special* to some right person. This craving almost totally preoccupies her. She spends most of her time in fantasizing a highly affectionate relationship with a special make-believe man. Though it has had no openly erotic expression, she has experienced considerable arousal. She feels guilty about it. This longing to be really special to some important person she sees as her paramount need in life.

Underlying Meaning: The desire to be special to an important person in one's life is healthy and normal. It is the intensity of her need which is fantasized toward a non-existent man that presents the problem. Unfortunately, the expectation is that she would not be able to sustain such a real relationship with a mature person. This is because any inclination she might have to give something of herself to another is overwhelmingly outweighed by her hunger to receive. Such a person's needs of this nature tend to be insatiable. Psychologically in this she is still more child than adult.

Suggestions On What To Do: As you listen to a person with this pattern of emotional problem you soon discover that in a number of important psychological areas, despite appearances, you are not dealing with an adult person. Thus you come to expect only the growth proper to a chronologically older person who is in some ways still a child. Professional help could benefit her(him). However, referral of such a person is a most delicate matter. She knows that she is not 'crazy'. Do you tell her that she is still a child? What answer could you give to her question,

"Why am I being referred for professional help?" Perhaps the best you can do is endeavor to explain that you do not feel qualified to help her with this which she sees as her primary need. Hence while you are seeing her in spiritual direction you wish she would also see someone thus qualified.

12. Aloneness

Difficulties Presented: [young single woman] She remarked she is not sure anyone understands how she feels. She is so alone. When she tries to explain some of her feelings and behaviors to others they do not seem to really comprehend what she is talking about. This leaves her feeling hurt, depressed and somewhat angry. When she looks deeply within herself what does she find? She beholds a person filled with needs to be accepted, to be affirmed, to be approved of, to be appreciated, to be loved, to receive affection. She is very aware that to act on these needs leaves her most vulnerable. Above all, she pointed out, she must first look to God for the fulfillment of these needs.

Underlying Meaning: The emotional hungers here stem from such a person's early childhood and carry with them childlike characteristics. Such hungers will never be adequately fulfilled or satisfied solely by a spiritual direction relationship.

Suggestions On What To Do: Normally it will take some time before a person with these needs will reveal them to you. By that time, presumably, a good rapport will have been established. Hence she(he) will be inclined to trust you as much as she could trust anyone. Then cautiously and gently as possible, you would be wise to discuss with her a possibility. It is that of getting, in addition to the spiritual direction, some assistance from one well versed professionally in helping with human needs.

Should professional help prove not feasible, such a person might benefit with a TRUSTED LISTENER (cf. Author's Foreword). In this relationship she could feel affirmed, accepted and appreciated. This could enable her to become gradually freed from her self-preoccupation and so begin to live for others.

13. Anger

Difficulties Presented: [young single woman] Obviously in a fury, she said she is very angry at God for not confirming her judgment that it is right for her to carry on her affair with a married man. She readily admits that she is sorry for the innocent persons she has thus hurt. Otherwise she feels absolutely no sorrow or guilt for what she has been doing, and so states that it must not be wrong. She thinks that she might have to give this man up, but not because it is morally wrong.

Underlying Meaning: A person with this type of difficulty is not yet ready to recognize her moral obligation to terminate such a relationship. This is because she is not now willing to give it up. Until she is, her psyche protects her from having to face that reality. Though she has no suspicion of what is going on, until she feels sorrow and guilt she will not have to face her obligation to discontinue this relationship.

Suggestions On What To Do: This kind of person unknowingly has her(his) defenses up. She cannot afford now to hear anything you have to say that would sound in any way judgmental of her behavior. The best thing I think you can do is to continue to listen patiently, without getting involved in her problem. Gradually she will come to feel that she is not alone. There is another who cares and understands. Moreover, it is one who respects her right to work her way through this highly personal problem. In addition to the grace present, her experience of such warm support will enable her to function at her best. After she has openly faced the whole reality of her situation, her anger against God will begin to lessen. Finally it should be noted that this should not be expected to happen in a day or so. It could take a number of months. If you think she is open to the suggestion that she consider looking for a TRUSTED LISTENER (cf. Author's Foreword), you might well suggest it. Such a one could be very helpful to her in her working through this problem area.

14. Anger

Difficulties Presented: [older woman religious] This woman is bitter. Her account is that she has worked like a slave all her life. Now she is not sure she is needed. The politics in religious life disgust her. Those who threaten superiors with quitting, etc., get what they want. She and the rest of the obedient women were used. Her anger is almost as constant as her bitterness.

Underlying Meaning: Frustration and anger can be appropriate responses to experienced injustice and ingratitude. Bitterness, however, which leaves one soured on life, is not a mature response in an adult. The politics and injustice to which this type of person refers may be real. Is her response of anger a healthy, mature one, or could she quite unwittingly be displacing anger against someone else on to other persons? Or, for instance, could this be an unrecognized fear of personal disintegration or even annihilation? It may take some time for you to feel fairly certain about this, and it might be that she would never recognize it.

Suggestions On What To Do: Listen and pray. Endeavor to catch her(his) feelings of hurt, outrage, anger, etc., and endeavor to feel for her. Allow her to get these hurts out and to give vent to her outrage. When the time seems right, clarify for her that God can manage to get His work done, even when rank politics are at work in the midst of it. Show her that God can bring good even out of injustices. Reassure her that she is free to resent the injustices, as behaviors, but needs an abundance of God's grace to forgive the persons responsible. If she is unwilling or unable to listen to such considerations, you may have to look for the opportunity to try referring her for professional help. Meanwhile she could continue to come to you for spiritual direction.

15. Anger

Difficulties Presented: [younger, middle-aged priest] In the course of his 30 day retreat, this man, who had been making spiritual progress, came in mad. He said he was so angry he feared he might explode. What baffled him, he added, was that he did not have a clue about what or at whom he was angry.

Underlying Meaning: Can it happen that a person becomes very angry with no idea of why or at whom? Yes. At times people find they are very angry and yet have no idea whatever why or at whom they are angry. The human psyche is very protective. This man said that anger had flooded through him while he was making a contemplation of Christ's Transfiguration. Then he blurted out, "It was the same damn thing at the raising of the daughter of Jairus and again in the garden. Always the same threesome: Peter, James and John. Where the hell was Andrew?" He pointed out that Andrew was around first, and had called his 'kid brother' Simon(Peter) some time later. He felt that this was a pretty shabby way to conduct things—repeatedly to pass up

Andrew, while including his kid brother in the 'inner circle' of intimate friends. He then mentioned that, incidentally, his own middle name was Andrew. Sometime later it dawned on him that in the situation he had been contemplating, Andrew's treatment symbolized unmistakably the sum total of all the times he had been passed over or put down. He had been deeply hurt in this way many times. Now it was clear what he was mad about. But at whom? It had to be God and more specifically the Second Person Incarnate, Jesus Christ, who had been responsible for bypassing Andrew. Then he recognized, with something of a shock, at Whom he was mad. Then he saw that he had to forgive God and especially Jesus Christ for the painful humiliations he had been allowed to suffer all his life. He did that and thus was able to ask forgiveness for his own sins from Jesus Christ. That took care of it.

Suggestions On What To Do: Allow a very angry person who is unaware of the cause of the anger to talk at length. When it is off his(her) chest,usually that person will eventually respond to the grace to recognize the cause of the anger. If you have a very clear idea of the source of the anger you will wisely refrain from mentioning it. When the person is ready to cooperate with the grace given to view openly the source, that recognition will take place. To try to speed it up is perilous. Even if you are uncomfortable in the presence of a very angry person, your most helpful role is to listen. Once the person sees what the anger is about, you may judge what good spiritual advice is in order.

16. Anger

Difficulties Presented: [middle-aged, married man] The first time this man came he blurted out that he was mad, mad, mad, at his parents, God, his boss, his wife, people making noise or pressuring him in any way. He said the real reason he was so mad was because his parents were 'phony'. As a teenager he had shouted this at them. He added that as a result he shows respect neither for the personhood of others nor for his own personhood. "In fact," he remarked, "I don't know who I am." He was almost immersed in his anger.

Underlying Meaning: This man who lacked a sense of personal identity and responsibility, was a deeply disturbed man. Regardless of the underlying psychological explanations for his anger, the wild eyes and his whole appearance said this man needed professional help. The unmistakable impression was that there was something seriously wrong here. This was not an ordinary pattern of anger. It would not take a professional clinician to recognize this.

Suggestions On What To Do: Begin by listening to a person with this type of problem. After prayer, trust what you think you should do. No matter how uncomfortable you feel, simply do it as well as you can. This type of person is never easy to deal with. He(she) will give the impression of a powder keg ready to blow. You might tell him that you do not feel qualified to help one whose problem is an anger you do not understand, but you would, if he wishes, help find someone who would be so qualified. Do not continue to see him, irrespective of motive, if you judge that this is something you ought not do. The earlier you can refer him for professional help, the less likely he is to experience a profound rejection by you.

17. Anger

Difficulties Presented: [middle-aged, single woman] This person has been furious at God the Father for letting His Son suffer so excruciatingly. At the same time, while she is not angry with Christ, she can't get close to him or trust him. It all seems to her to center on the feeling that she can in no way accept Christ's sufferings. Even though she still feels angry with the Father, she pleaded with Him to help her and heard in reply a clear, "Let Me love you." She does not question the authentic nature of this answer, though she doesn't understand it. Although she has no memories of specific persons and events, she has somehow known for some time that as a young child she was physically, badly abused. And even though she does not recall what these hurtful experiences were, she knows she cannot yet forgive the persons responsible for them. Nor can she forgive herself for burdening and hurting her poor mother by her illness.

Underlying Meaning: Without any question it is her conviction that these angers, etc., of hers have their roots in experiences in her very early life. As she continues to explore her experiences she is recognizing that she is too *self-attending* and not enough *other-attending*. She mentioned that she is beginning to understand that Christ's suffering, which she cannot accept, symbolizes strikingly her own suffering, which she can neither accept nor forgive. I gradually became convinced that this person, one of the hurting ones, was being guided by the Holy Spirit, and showing notable spiritual and psychological growth.

Suggestions On What To Do: As you listen to the person with this type of difficulty you note that besides anger, one of her(his) great difficulties is being able to forgive others and herself. And even though you may judge that you do not have the training to help her with her anger, you still might assist her to advance spiritually by giving her help in forgiving. This you might do by showing her her own need for depending on God's grace and strength. Perhaps later still you might decide also to refer her for professional help for her anger.

18. Anger

Difficulties Presented: [younger, middle-aged, woman religious] She remarked that, in general, things seem to go along fairly well and then suddenly a rage surfaces. She is invariably surprised by its sudden onset. This is always followed by a depression. The reason for her anger, she said, is only too clear. "I'm furious at God because He summoned me to be a celibate. I really had no choice. As a woman I am smothered in religious life. Now that I'm close to the change of life, it's too late to have children of my own and even a man of my own, I suspect."

Underlying Meaning: The basic frustration of a woman in such a situation is that she does not feel free in religious life. The presumption here is that if there were any freedom in the original commitment of her vocation it was never internalized. Her surprising outbursts of anger appear to be the psychological outcries of a woman experiencing personal violation.

Suggestions On What To Do: Listening to a woman religious with this kind of difficulty as she gets it off her chest will give her some temporary relief. She really needs you to assist her through a *process of discernment* concerning her vocation. To do this, when you think she is strong enough for it, I think you would be justified in reassuring her that God does not want a slavish service from her. Tell her that *for the purpose of discernment* she may prescind from her religious vows and prayerfully regard herself *free* to choose the state of life in which she will live her life for God. Help her arrive *through discernment* at *freely* choosing either to remain in religious life or to leave religious life. Until she makes such a *discernment-based choice* she will not be a free woman and will continue to periodically experience personal violation.

19. Anger

Difficulties Presented: [younger, middle-aged, single woman] This woman, during a retreat, said she couldn't pray. She didn't seem to want to. And had no idea why. Her remark was she was just angry. "I'm not certain at whom. Probably at me and at God. He wants me to play by His rules. He didn't make me beautiful, brilliant and an entrancing person. If he had would I be what I am today? Probably not. I am angry at me. I can't forgive me. I can't. And I can't forgive others."

Underlying Meaning: This woman appeared to be revealing personal inadequacy and basic insecurity as well as questionable motivation for her present status in life. These sources could account for her deep frustrations. Much of her anger she appeared to have turned in on herself. Although she had not specifically mentioned depression I would assume that she has had painful and not infrequent bouts with it as well as with anxiety. Self-hatred was also being indicated. Something that is not yet manifest underlies her problem with forgiveness, especially of herself.

Suggestions On What To Do: Continued listening in a caring way may be all you can do if you see such a person only for a short time. If it is for a longer period, she(he) may eventually reveal to you the grounds for her anger at self, even if as yet she is not aware of the real grounds for being angry. Should she make such revelations, which she could do without even being aware that she was revealing anything, you might be able, through spiritual direction, to help her. Moreover, her insistence that she cannot forgive herself would seem to signal something that could benefit from the right professional support. With this type of problem you need great patience and the courage to remind yourself that when in doubt, listen. If you would feel that she might need psychological help as well, and the right professional help was not possible, what then? You might suggest that she consider seeking a TRUSTED LISTENER (cf. Author's Foreword).

20. Anger

Difficulties Presented: [middle-aged, single woman] She reported that she has gone for professional counseling, off and on, for years, but it has not helped her. As a child she had lived in poverty. Looking back, she sees that she was always trailing others in every way, and was even very late in reaching puberty. As a girl she had been afflicted with migraine headaches, especially while visiting friends. At these times she became so sick that she would leave the table and disgorge her food. She had begun to get very angry at others and couldn't afford to show it, so she pushed the anger down within herself. Now she knows she has to deal with her reservoir of anger in order to have a healthy spiritual life. She noted she has read dozens of books on psychology none of which has helped her.

Underlying Meaning: She mentioned that her anger was not directed at her father for the wretched poverty. "It would be unfair to blame my father, a loving man, for not being a better provider. He tried and tried but always came up short. I could have been angry at God." She said she now knows that her anger comes from her lack of true humility, because her failures invariably lessen her self-concept and make her mad. She knows she is not yet healed. Her further insight is that some of her anger comes from jealousy of God's gifts to other people. She is also angry at God as well as at them for that. This analysis, as far as it goes, appears to be accurate.

Suggestions On What To Do: Among the dozens of books she had read she found passages on how to deal with anger. She was advised to get rid of her anger by displacing it. Beat a pillar with a rubber hose. Hit extra hard in a contact sport. Scream at the top of your lungs. Imagine you are doing these things to the person you hate, etc. These can all be helpful in terms of giving temporary relief. They can be good first aid. That is all. They do not get at the source of the anger. Anger comes not from things but from persons. I can get frustrated at something. I get angry only at someone. The one I get really angry at is the one I care about. And implicitly, at least, I make the judgment that the one who has done something hurtful to me did so knowingly and willingly. My most intense anger appears to come when someone has publicly humiliated, belittled, done a real put down on me. If you could prove to me that the person who did this hurtful thing to me was sleepwalking at the time he did it, my anger would have no source from which to well up. The only way I know of to get rid of the source of anger is this. First, beg God for the grace to forgive this person. Then, in prayer, go in imagination with Jesus Christ, and *forgive* this person. It may be necessary to do this more than once. This dries up the source of the anger. Professional counseling, thus far at least, has not helped much. Listen patiently to this type of person as she(he) talks on and on. Don't be surprised if she displaces her anger, for a time, on you her spiritual director. Understand that she is relieved at being able to get it off her back and lay it on someone, safely. If she pressures you to play the clinician, gently but firmly refuse to do so. Understand that she will seldom be able to talk about her spiritual growth without talking about her psychological problems. Let her learn by experience that you are there just listening. After some months you should be able to judge whether or not she also needs to try professional help again. My impression is that she is in need of the right professional help. If she would not consider this you might encourage her to look for one who could be a TRUSTED LISTENER (cf. Author's Foreword). She might thus receive some help.

21. Anger

Difficulties Presented: [middle-aged, single woman] During a 30 day retreat she remarked that she was not on very good terms with God. She had precious little hope for the future and no trust whatever in Him. She was good and mad at Him, she said, for all He had allowed to happen to her and her loved ones. In fact this retreat was kind of a last chance she was giving Him to straighten out and do right by her and hers.

Underlying Meaning: There might have been other unconscious factors operative here. What came to the fore was her anger. There was no way she could accept that a just, merciful God could have allowed such suffering and distress to her and those she loved. She had Him so far back in the doghouse that she would not let Him touch her. She needed a great deal of grace to forgive God for what she could neither understand nor accept.

Suggestions On What To Do: After listening during several sessions ask such a person to go to the God she(he) is mad at and say something like, "Help! Even though I'm mad at You, please help me! I don't even know what to ask You for." Later you may need to help her see that she first has to forgive God, for which she will need much grace. This she can do in private prayer, perhaps employing her imagination. Once she has forgiven Him, she will then be in a position to go to Him for forgiveness. For this she also will need great grace. Tell her you will pray for her. Sooner or later she will receive undeniable graces, during which she will be able to see clearly, and see through, what she had feared. She will find that trust of God is a by-product of her awareness of His personal love for her, rather than something she prays for. These should be the hallmarks of her spiritual growth. In the case of this single woman, she was able to forgive

God and that was the beginning of having her problems taken care of.

22. Anger

Difficulties Presented: [younger married woman] Now, this woman said, she can understand the motivation of those people who hurt her during her childhood. At least she knows that each of them had his or her own problems with which to be preoccupied. So, not surprisingly they could not give her much consideration. Besides, she remembers that she did not really get mad at them in the first place. She couldn't afford to. Instead she turned the anger in on herself, telling herself that she was no good and deserved even more hurt than she was getting from them. It puzzles her now to be aware that she is very angry at each of them for what they did to her.

Underlying Meaning: She is finding out that anger turned in on self and thus pushed down does not go away. Neither is it dissipated by the person's understanding it in adulthood. Rather it maintains itself as unfinished business until the person concerned is psychologically strong enough to let it surface and begin to cope with it. The hurts that produced such anger are still there within her, together with their childhood responses. In a word, some of these hurts are almost devastating. The anger is proportionately intense, carrying with it the urge to destroy. In order to deal with her anger in a healthy manner, she needs to be freed to redirect it from herself to those she sees as responsible. This means identifying the persons at whom she is angry, not necessarily expressing her anger at them. As long as she bottled it up by directing it against herself, she was safe but in an unhealthy way.

Suggestions On What To Do: Tell her(him) that she needs a tremendous amount of grace even to begin to deal with this area. The fact that she has now become aware of this anger is a healthy sign. It says that she is psychologically prepared to start to deal with these accumulated angers and that God's grace is there. She needs to ask for great grace *in order to forgive these people*. In time you will be able to show her how to do that. In imagination, together with Jesus Christ and with his strength she will go to each of these persons *with* and *for* Christ to forgive each of them. She may need to do this more than once especially with some of these people. Over a period of time she should be thus freed of these long hidden but nonetheless operative angers. She could need professional help as well.

23. Avoidance

Difficulties Presented: [middle-aged, married man] After a number of remarks to get a bit comfortable, this man began to talk about his family, of whom he said he was proud. Then he remarked, "Of course I don't talk to my wife. I've found that's the only way we can live in peace." It wasn't clear to me what he meant by that remark, so he explained, "For instance, when I want something at the table, I ask one of the children, 'will you please ask your mother to pass the butter?' I discovered many months ago that the only possibility of reasonably peaceful coexistence is to disregard her as completely as possible. As long as she does not exist in my life things are tolerable."

Underlying Meaning: The pattern of avoidance rather than calm confrontation and clarification in interpersonal problems has proven most hurtful. People who habitually confront others quietly in difficulties become aware of how easily one can misinterpret another's motivation. We spontaneously ascribe motivations especially to the hurtful actions or omissions of others. For instance, a man can readily misread the motivation of a woman's action. He is using a man's norm, which does not fit her. A woman can easily misjudge especially an omission on the part of a man. She is using a woman's yardstick to measure, and it is not suitable for him. Ignoring another's existence as far as possible is a psychologically unhealthy pattern. It could be indicative of serious underlying emotional problems.

Suggestions On What To Do: After a good deal of listening you may pick up the source of the pattern of avoidance. It may appear to be something the person has learned from early childhood. If so it is conceivable that the person could, with your help and support, begin to change the pattern. If the person insists on justifying the avoidance, or otherwise resists any thought of changing it, presume the person has a serious problem calling for professional help. In the case mentioned above, some marriage counseling would give the two parents the actual opportunity of beginning to talk together. This, which is of the utmost importance, is impossible at home. Spiritual direction combined with professional help can be very promising. Spiritual help by itself could be ill-advised.

24. Awakening

Difficulties Presented: [young woman religious] This young woman said she became suddenly aware of her almost consuming hunger to have a child, to experience motherhood. She became conscious of being depressed, as well. Sometime later she met a wonderful man and began to fall in love with him. She was surprised how strong her affectionate attraction together with physical arousal towards him was.

Underlying Meaning: This appears to be her twofold awakening as a woman and as a mother. She may not have been saying it to me correctly. Often a woman's longing is not just to have a child, but to have this *particular* man's child. Probably the depression results from her feeling 'caught' in vowed celibacy by her conscience. Many a religious realizes only later that when she pronounced vows there was no full realization of what she was surrendering. Accordingly it later becomes an occasion for a choice. The person asks, "Is God calling me to this kind of life?" If the answer is affirmative, it presents the opportunity to give a greater expression of her love to God. If the answer appears very doubtful, then when you judge the person is ready she should begin a process of discernment. Its purpose is to discover in what state of life God wants her to lead her life for Him, and in what state of life she wants to live her life for God.

Suggestions On What To Do: In the face of these new realizations such a person must come to terms with her(his) vocation. Listen to her and be with her as she endeavors to work her way through this vocation crisis. I think you ought not take a position and persuade her of the correctness of that position. Simply be with her so that she does not have to undertake this all by herself. Especially give her a process of discernment to follow so that she will be peaceful and satisfied with the conclusion she reaches.

25. Belonging

Difficulties Presented: (middle-aged, woman religious) For some years this woman, whom I directed in a retreat, has faithfully, she said, continued with her work despite continuing frustration. She has been trying, without success, to disregard some of the painful realities that have become a part of her life.

Among these latter is her aching to do God's will while feeling that her present work is not doing that. She gets along well enough with people both in and out of religious life. Still she feels that she actually belongs no place. She has not felt at home anywhere in years. It is pretty much a matter of forcing herself into and through each day. She asks, "What does God want me to do? Where does He want me to be? Somehow I don't feel I am where He wants me to be. I pray and no answers come. Meanwhile in trying to do what I am doing where I am, I am miserable."

Underlying Meaning: Such a person could be indicating insecurity or even inadequacy. Yet it need not be either. Clearly there is more going on here than appears on the surface. Something within her, which she does not even suspect, is fighting tooth and nail against her present situation. It might, for instance be that she is indicating affection starvation. It could be that she lacks security and its attendant flexibility. In the short time she was seeing me I did not spot what her basic problem was.

Suggestions On What To Do: This is the kind of situation where you could well see yourself primarily in the role of a prayer companion. Suggest that over a period of several weeks you both storm heaven. Ask God to help her(him) and help you to help her if that is what He wants. Leave God free to answer your prayers in any way He chooses. In addition, suggest to her that from time to time she might simply open the scriptures anywhere, and for a few minutes let God talk to her. When you think the time is right you might ask her how she sees God communicating to her through obedience. At the right time you might also ask her to consider receiving some professional assistance while she continues with you in spiritual direction.

26. Bitterness

Difficulties Presented: [middle-aged, woman religious] During her directed retreat, it took this woman some time to get beyond the stage of making polite conversation. She then acknowledged that she constantly carries a load of bitterness. When she has tried to explain to herself why she feels so bitter, a number of things have come to mind. "Why have I not had the wonderful spiritual experiences other women religious describe? I have been terribly hurt by the injustices and manipulation suffered at the hands of superiors. I feel nauseous when I think of how often superiors have said to me, 'I know your great faith will enable you to see the will of God in this.' Whose will?" She insists she has been used by numberless people, religious and others.

Underlying Meaning: It comes as no surprise that some religious have been hurt in religious life. But after a few visits I began to get the impression that this was something else. It seemed more to be the cumulative result of her having nurtured negative psychological responses to hurts over the years. These included envy, some depersonalization, fears, etc. I sensed a thinly disguised personality inadequacy. Quite unwittingly she appeared to be blaming her problems and troubles on others.

Suggestions On What To Do: Your close listening to such a person usually will begin to reveal some inkling whether or not this is pathological. If it is not, she(he) finds she is not alone and has in you a sympathetic, listening other person. Thus she should be gradually freed to view some of these hurtful happenings in her life in a way that will enable her to begin to cope with them. In time, some explanation can be of help. For instance, you could explain to her that resentment, anger and disappointment are appropriate responses to unfair, unjust treatment, while bitterness is not. And the resentment is resentment of the *behavior* and not of the *person*. Thus she can in private prayer, with God's grace, forgive the persons. She may also continue to resent such treatment regardless of from whom it comes and who is receiving it. Following this forgiveness her anger should subside, even though her resentment of such behavior would persist. However, if you begin to sense, as I did with this woman, that something deeper is really wrong here, then what? Then accept it that she is in need of professional help. Incidentally, it might be of assistance to you to know that if this is pathological, the anticipation is that this pattern yields only very slowly to therapy.

27. Busy

Difficulties Presented: [middle-aged, married man] During the first session this man explained that he does not even have time for his family, let alone time to pray. He is, he said, on his way up the executive ladder in his company. The competition is fierce. This is an eighteen hour a day job. It is a matter of arriving early, leaving late, meeting the 'right' people, reading the 'right' publications, etc. He laughed as he said that he should be reintroduced to his family. He is sorry but added that he needs to make big money and there is no other way for him to get it. He asked, "What about spiritual direction, say about once a month for ten minutes? But no praying in between visits. There is simply no time for it."

Underlying Meaning: In our society this man is not all that different from a good number of people. You would wonder that he seems not to have questioned his priorities. He had the marks of a driven man. Why does he have to have big money at such a price? Does his wife demand it? At best his motivation is both spiritually and psychologically unhealthy. At worst, psychologically this could be an ill man.

Suggestions On What To Do: This man could not afford to 'waste' the time needed to talk to a spiritual director. Ten minutes a month simply would not do. Should you sense that he(she) needs professional help as well as spiritual direction, what could you tell him? Perhaps you could mention that the right professional help would help him get unwound. Moreover it did not make good business sense to pass up first class help for personal tension. At any rate, it would not be a prudent move on your part to let him specify the terms of the spiritual direction sessions.

28. Clinical Failures

Difficulties Presented: [later middle-aged, married man] As soon as this man came he said that he had gone to psychologists and psychiatrists for years and received no help. The answer to his personal problems, he felt, lay not in therapy but in spiritual direction. There was no mistaking the point that he did not appear to be psychologically healthy.

Underlying Meaning: It is not clear why certain emotionally disturbed persons fail to improve in therapy. Some of them may have had clinicians who were wrong for them. What is clear is that it is not the proper role of a spiritual director to help such people back to health.

Suggestions On What To Do: As early as possible tell such a person, who is unwilling to consider further therapy, something such as the following. "With my limited knowledge of feelings and emotional problems I am convinced that God does not want me to be your spiritual director." Do not let the person force you into a therapy role under the appearance of spiritual direction.

29. Commitment

Difficulties Presented: [young, single man] A seminarian, he says that as far as he can see here and now he wants to be a priest. He explains that he would not be so presumptuous as to attempt to predict the future, for only God knows the future. And God expects him to be a responsible person. He is old enough, he explains, to realize that situations or circumstances can happen that would make a lifetime commitment of any kind simply impossible. Any such commitment, he pointed out, could constitute a violation of his nature and of his person. He prays that such will not be the case, but insists that in no way can he rule out the possibility. He declared that the same thing, of course, would have to hold true for a lifetime commitment in marriage.

Underlying Meaning: At first hearing this may sound like an intelligent, reasonable position. We live in a throw-away culture. Everything from cigarette lighters and flashlights to table utensils are meant to be used and thrown away. There is increasing absence of the permanent, the unchanging, the invariable in our lives. Yet additional reflection indicates that his is a faithless position. A person of faith commits himself or herself to God with the underlying trust that although it is impossible for us to predict the future, God, in His love, will see us through every obstacle. That never means that it will be easy. It means that with His grace it will be possible and in so doing we will never be wiped out as persons. This holds for every life commitment made in love to God. It appears to be safe to assume the presence in his life of a deep insecurity. He simply must keep the controls. He is certain that God wants him to be responsible for his free choices. Any other course, in his eyes, would probably be a 'copout'. He is sure that God does not want him to act irresponsibly even under the garb of faith.

Suggestions On What To Do: I would tend to think that spiritual direction, by itself, holds little promise of helping such a person. He(she)will find the complete trust implicit in permanent commitment repugnant. You ought ultimately to trust your own impressions regarding whether you can help such a person, should he balk at the mention of the right professional help.

30. Confession

Difficulties Presented: [younger, middle-aged, woman religious] I have known this woman since she was a freshman in college. Off and on during the intervening years I have been her spiritual director. She is a very good person, intelligent, a committed religious, generous, prayerful, obedient and apostolic. Recently she mentioned to me that a group of women religious no longer receive the sacrament of reconciliation in private confession. Their reason: "They don't feel that it really has any significant meaning for them." If they encounter a well done reconciliation liturgy they may receive the sacrament. Now she says she is beginning to take the same position. Some of them have gone for over a year without this sacrament. I have no reason to suppose that these are not very good women, who regard themselves, in God's eyes, as fine religious.

Underlying Meaning: I try, without much success, to find value in this stance. Yet I see them as missing opportunities for beautiful personal encounters with Jesus Christ. I frankly do not comprehend this position. I know that to reason with one of these women would be of no avail. Much of my difficulty in appreciating fully this attitude, I suspect, comes from the fact that I am a man. My hunch is that the right woman religious spiritual director would know what to do.

Suggestions On What To Do: I find I am somewhat baffled. My sense is that she would not accept a referral to a woman spiritual director. To mention it could only hurt her. Yet I find nothing in the New Code of Canon Law to substantiate this attitude. In fact, Canon 960 reads, "Individual and integral confession and absolution constitute the only ordinary way by which the ordinary person who is aware of serious sin is reconciled with God and the Church." And Canon 989 speaks of individual confession as obligatory for "...serious sins at least once a year." Of course both Canons speak of *serious* sin. I would assume that at least most of these women are familiar with these Canons. I think I would tell one of these women that I am not comfortable with that position. Beyond that it is not clear what I should say.

31. Confirmation

Difficulties Presented: [later middle-aged, married man] This man referred to himself, during a retreat, as a charismatic Catholic. He reported that while he was praying he had an inspiration to begin to undertake a special work for God. He then asked the Spirit for confirmation of his prayer. Almost immediately, he said, he began to shake out of control so that the coins in his pants pocket jingled. He then asked Christ for confirmation. Immediately, he added, there was a reduced, quiet trembling. Later in the day he again asked the Spirit for confirmation and again began to shake out of control. He regards these as unmistakable confirmations by God that he is to begin this work.

Underlying Meaning: It was very important to him that I understood immediately that he was a charismatic Catholic. Hence I was not surprised that the Divine 'confirmations' most receptive to him would be largely sensory in nature. At the same time, I think many spiritual directors would join me in being somewhat skeptical about the authenticity of such 'confirmations'.

Suggestions On What To Do: At the time this man reported these experiences I felt that he was not open to any questioning of their genuineness. In your dealing with such a person what ought you to do? When you sensed the time to be right, you might explain to him(her) that no one can predict what form God's confirmation will take. At the same time it might be wise to ask God for confirmation that could not be so readily challenged as the product of some kind of auto-suggestion. If he insists on the authenticity of these 'signs' (e.g., shaking) of God's confirmation, you know what type of person you are dealing with. You might have to tell him that you are not comfortable in acting as his spiritual director.

32. Confusion

Difficulties Presented: [young woman religious] Near the end of her retreat she wrote, "I can't sleep anyway, so I might as well get this off my chest. When we were sitting around (Monday night) and I was down on solid earth again, human respect whispered, 'What a silly sap you've been!' but I decided to accept the humiliation and forget about it, and just crawl back into the safety of my hideaway. No more manifestation of conscience for me. It didn't work. Instead I wanted you to really understand what I was having such great difficulty in trying to tell you. Father, if I'm just going 'whackey' please tell me. Retreat is over. You've been very patient and I thank you. There's a probability that you really do understand and that I'm the dumb bunny who doesn't realize that other people are able to talk these things over very freely with each other with no embarrassment whatsoever.

"For a moment, may I be the me that nobody sees and talk sentimental nonsense? I have been asking Christ to manifest His love in some tangible way. I had no right to this after the way I've treated Him. Not that I did anything awful. If I may say this without being irreverent a limping comparison would be that of a wife refusing to give herself completely to her husband even though she dutifully performed all of her other duties conscientiously. He is my ALL. I live from one Communion to the next; nothing else matters. And yet here was the contradiction—I don't like people. I don't enjoy being around them. If my love for Christ were wholesome, I would *love* people, wouldn't I?

"And then here, during retreat, (May I be more silly and sentimental yet? No, I haven't been reading too many love stories and living vicariously.) The Risen Christ takes me into His arms and presses me *close* to His Sacred Heart. Yes, it was sweet while it lasted, but I can't go around mooning about it. I should be proving my love by deeds. I don't want my so-called love for others to be artificial and superficial. That's why I guess I'll have to play it cool until He puts the real thing into my heart. Otherwise it's too phony. Being a 'charitable' gadabout turns me off.

"Some day, when you have time, can you tell me whether you think I'm on the right track? Or am I rationalizing and stalling? When the time comes He is capable of picking me up and putting me where He wants me."

Underlying Meaning: A most important element in the relationship to one's spiritual director is the feeling-conviction that regardless of what the latter hears, "He will in no way think less of me." For some people, eight days of a retreat are not nearly long enough to establish such trust. This woman still feels like a 'silly sap'. What she seems to be accusing herself of in terms of her 'artificial love' for others is a culpable absence of unconditional surrender to Christ. (Thus her comparison with the wife refusing to give herself completely to her husband.) That she does not want to be phony in her love relationships to people is good. She has however identified *love with feelings*. This false identification can be corrected. On the basis of the impressions of her gathered during eight days, I would not out of hand reject the genuineness of her experience of Christ's taking her into His arms.

Suggestions On What To Do: Parenthetically, I answer letters of this kind to let the person know that I read them and think I understand, but I do not attempt spiritual direction through correspondence. For me spiritual direction calls for personal presence. Assuming, then, ongoing personal contact with such a person, I suggest the following. If you accept and respect the person irrespective of her(his) reported behavior (on which incidentally you are seldom asked to pass judgment) that acceptance will get through. It takes as much time as it takes. I know of no instant friendship, no instant acceptance, no instant trust, etc. All these take time. Show the person that love consists not in feelings but in actions. The amount of one's love for another is not the depth of the feelings but what one is willing to do, at personal sacrifice, for the other. "Greater love than this no man has that a man lay down his life for another." Most important is to accept her as she is. It may be helpful to explain to her that she has no obligation whatever to let every person know her intimately. Instead she may carefully pick her close friends, those with whom she chooses to share what is most personal. For most people this is but one or two persons. She is to love people along the whole gamut of those she knows, ranging from enemies through mere acquaintances, to closest friends. There is nothing phony about really loving those whom she would never want to have as close friends. Finally, tell her that her regret about lacking unconditional surrender to Christ is most understandable. But assure her that with all her generosity she still needs a great amount of His helping grace to accomplish such a surrender. The right kind of professional person might benefit her.

33. Criticism

Difficulties Presented: [middle-aged, single man] This man spoke with intense feelings about his being very critical of God's world, with its inequalities, injustices, sufferings, abandoned street people, etc. He has endeavored to pray but simply cannot force himself even to try to pray to God, especially as Father. This he does not understand and it bothers him considerably.

Underlying Meaning: His "criticism" appears to be an un-recognized expression of resentment and anger. This might be a displaced hostility. Very often this kind of problem stems from an early intensely hurtful relationship with one's own father. Such a person often cannot psychologically afford to face the rejection by his father. Nonetheless he will spontaneously tend to counterreject, probably in a way or ways which conceal from him what he is doing. It would seem that this man could not afford to recognize that his 'criticism' might be a counterrejection of his own rejecting father which he has, without being aware of it, dis-placed onto God the Father of the world and his Father.

Suggestions On What To Do: You may be able very deli-cately to help this type of person help himself(herself). The man needs to become aware of what his 'criticism' is really saying. Then, after asking for God's special help, in prayerful imagina-tion he needs to confront and forgive his father. Then he will be in a position to ask his father's forgiveness. Next he could repeat the same with God his Father. Either or both of these may have to be done more than once, before the person concerned is wholly freed from the hostility.

34. Dependency

Difficulties Presented: [middle-aged, married man] My understanding that his mother has unbelievably good judgment was important to this man. In fact, he added, he has never made a decision of any substance about anything without consulting her. His wife came to see me and told me that his mother makes his decisions and that he couldn't dream of going against what she decides in anything. Then his wife appended the following information. His occupational record is extremely poor and he manages money very badly. He invariably goes to his financially well-to-do mother for money whenever he gets in financial straits. Later, he volunteered to me that he gets money from his mother when he is short, and asked, "What's wrong with that? She is my mother, after all." He mentioned that he had had a number of well paying jobs, which he rather enjoyed, but said he quit each one of them because, "My mother didn't go for it."

Underlying Meaning: He increasingly gave the impression of a chronological adult functioning at the psychological level of about a 12 year old. His wife realizes clearly that she is married to a 48 year old boy. She has settled for that reality. The children, she is sure, in their own way also realize this though she has never discussed it with them.

Suggestions On What To Do: You might try to refer him(her) for professional assistance. You could expect to find this most difficult. With the mind-set of a boy he sees nothing whatever improper or immature in his behavior or attitudes. If you choose to take him on for spiritual direction, expect that you will at times experience a good deal of frustration and disappointment.

35. Depression

Difficulties Presented: [younger single woman] This woman insisted that her continuous depression was the product of what she viewed as her compulsive pattern of sin. She had tried to break this pattern but all in vain. She had even found a couple of confessors, she said, who had told her it was not seriously sinful, if indeed sinful at all, and to pay little attention to such happenings. She said that in a way she appreciated what they were trying to do, but could not quite accept their moral positions.

Underlying Meaning: Such a problem could have any one of a number of different foundational meanings.

Suggestions On What To Do: You might point out to a person with such a problem the importance of viewing her(his) every failure as a cue to her *need* for Jesus Christ. Her record shows her she really cannot adequately handle this problem even with great generosity. Why not turn it over to Him? Then she could be encouraged to ask Him to show her what this problem is really saying, to let her comprehend its meaning if this is His will. It is of the utmost importance that she understand that after she shares this knowledge, you in no way think less of her. Later you would be in a better position to see if she has need for professional assistance.

36. Depression

Difficulties Presented: [younger middle-aged, single woman] Her story was that she has lived with constant depression for years. After almost endless soul-searching her conclusion is that she has no idea whatever why she is depressed.

She characterizes herself as timid and yet turbulent within, but above all mired in depression.

Underlying Meaning: When dealing with a depressed person it is always important to consider first the possibility of an organic source. Because this depression is constant in the case of this woman, it does not appear to be tied, at least primarily, to her menstrual cycle. After a thorough medical examination had produced negative results, how would the depression be explained? This is anything but obvious. My own theory (which to my knowledge no one else has confirmed or even proposed), drawn from years of counseling experience is this. The feeling of depression is produced by the experience, almost always below the level of awareness, of the person's being trapped (caught, enslaved, or helplessly entangled). In what? In a *personally unacceptable situation.* This situation produces the experience of personal violation. That which binds the person in this unbearable state of affairs may be any one of a number of things. It may be fear in one who is afraid to break out and try to go it alone, or leave because of threats. It may be conscience in one who does not believe that escape is morally permissible. For instance, one does not believe in divorce and is caught in an impossible marriage. Again, the means of getting out of any intolerable situation may be felt to be wrong. It may be one's basic conviction that, for a grave reason, a specific condition must be endured regardless of personal cost. It may be the utter frustration of having to accept the inability to achieve a hungered-for goal. It may be that the price to be paid for what is yearned for is seen as far too high. It may be the recognition of being caught in an intolerable situation from which one is physically unable to escape. It may be the conviction that it is too late for escape.

Suggestions On What To Do: Encourage the person to have a medical examination. Assuming there were negative findings, I would propose the following. As you listen at length you may begin to spot what the impossible situation is, and what is binding the person in it. If you do so, the strong likelihood is that the depressed person will have no conception of this situation, at least as a source of depression. In fact were this to be mentioned to her(him), the reply might well be, "Impossible situation? What do you mean?" You would wisely assume that this person now cannot afford psychologically to face this explanation of the depression as true. As you allow her to talk on, however, she could begin to see this explanation. This is because she has the strength coming from being able to share this with you in addition to God's grace. Delicately you might even ask, if she really has mentioned it, "Are you saying that you feel somehow trapped?" After this person has clearly faced it, feel your way to examine with her whether or not it *needs* to be viewed as an impossible situation. If so, then you may want gently to help her look at the trap which is imprisoning her. See if there might be other options open to her.

37. Depression

Difficulties Presented: [middle-aged, married woman] The first time this woman who appeared to be in her late forties came she was badly depressed. She said she had been thinking of taking her life, and wondered if spiritual direction from a priest might help her. She was excessively restless. Almost immediately, pacing the floor and gesturing wildly, she began to speak of her unforgivable sin of having arranged for the murder of her unborn baby. She asked, "Don't you understand? I had my baby killed." This which had happened many years ago, she said, had now returned to haunt her night and day.

Underlying Meaning: This whole pattern of excited, agitated depression, with the deep sense of her unforgivable sin, had the appearance of a mental-emotional illness which a few women develop at the change of life. Fortunately it usually responds well to medication. It calls for referral to a psychiatrist.

Suggestions On What To Do: Try to refer such a woman for psychiatric help as early as possible. The anticipation is that such a referral can be accomplished only with the assistance of her family. Until she receives such professional help spiritual direction would be out of the question.

38. Depression

Difficulties Presented: [middle-aged, woman religious] This woman said she is now living in depression. She formerly held a very important position in her religious community and also was prominent in the local civic community. She has recently been given a position contacting the public in which she is 'teamed up' with a very powerful personality who comes on strong. When they meet socially and professionally important people, she feels they do not even notice her, so overwhelming is the presence of this other woman. Constantly she senses that she lives in this woman's shadow. The jealousy she feels tortures and mortifies her, leaving her feeling very guilty. All of which seems to reinforce the depression.

Underlying Meaning: I became convinced that her depression did not stem from something pathological that was concealed from her. It seemed to betray some hitherto unsuspected personal inadequacy. For this highly gifted woman, just to acknowledge that she could and actually did experience jealousy of another woman was a thoroughly disconcerting and most embarrassing admission. She was experiencing an appropriate feeling in perceiving that in the presence of this other striking woman, people of some stature did not even notice her.

Suggestions On What To Do: A person with this kind of difficulty could gently be led to understand that she(he) is free to talk about it as much as she wants. In time she might be brought to see that the situation, though painful, is not impossible to accept. With God's grace she can carry this cross for Jesus Christ. Moreover, if she is a generous person she might be led to a higher spiritual level. Without giving occasion for it, she could welcome being passed over and regarded as a nobody in order to be more like her suffering Savior. Either of these should take care of her problem. The willingness to carry this cross for Him or the acceptance and even welcoming of her being ignored should have the effect of reducing the depression. A TRUSTED LISTENER (cf. Author's Foreword) could prove very beneficial to such a woman.

39. Depression

Difficulties Presented: [middle-aged single woman] Almost immediately she reported that she is constantly depressed. She remarked that she really doesn't know why. Continually she hungers to be loved and to receive warm, comforting affection particularly from certain people. In her affection-starvation she is preoccupied in the search for love. Yet, she knows that even were love offered to her there is no way she could accept it as love. To be able to accept it at all she would have to view it as something other than love. In so doing she would automatically strip it of its power to satisfy her hunger. And she lives on in depression.

Underlying Meaning: This not uncommon pattern of depression seems to indicate a psychological aftermath of very early affection deprivation. As such it is pathological and signals a need for professional assistance. She is demonstrating the psychological finding that in order to be able to love, a child must first be loved. This woman could not accept an expression of warmth from another *as love,* because she feels certain she is *not lovable.*

Suggestions On What To Do: It would be perilous to· endeavor to try to help solely with spiritual direction, a person presenting this kind of problem. Your challenge rather, is the delicate one of conveying to her(him) that you would be most uncomfortable in trying to help her with her depression since you have not been trained along these lines. At the same time you will be glad to give her spiritual direction in other areas if she would also see someone who is professionally qualified to assist her in dealing with her depression.

40. Depression

Difficulties Presented: [younger middle-aged, single woman] Maintaining that she suffers constantly from depression, she added that she knows why she is depressed. All her life she has longed for God's love and respect but that is impossible because He knows without a doubt what a phony she is. Formerly she had her mother's love and especially respect and that helped. Now that her mother is in heaven she too knows what a phony her daughter is.

Underlying Meaning: She is giving clear signals of a badly damaged self-concept. In addition, the mistaken conviction that she must live up to the expectations of the one whose love she longs for is not changed simply by receiving correct information. Neither of these difficulties will be helped solely by spiritual direction.

Suggestions On What To Do: Compassionately you could be strongly inclined to try to show a person with such a pattern that she(he) is not really phony and that God does love her. Your attempt would be fruitless. Indeed, should you yield to this temptation you might find not only that she is no longer able to talk to you, but may wonder whether you would have further damaged her. Rather, tell her that while she is receiving some professional help with her depression you will be glad to be her spiritual director. In that role endeavor to stay clear of this whole area of correcting her erroneous notions.

41. Destructive Association

Difficulties Presented: (older woman religious) In something of a depressed state this woman reported that her superior had talked to her about moving her. Being moved was not a problem for her. What was bothering her was that her superior spoke of assigning her to live with a member of the community who, she feels certain, could destroy her as a person. Often she has asked herself why this should be so. She doesn't know if this other person hates her for something of which she is not aware, or simply regards her as a nonentity. What she does know is that this person has always had a devastating effect on her. She is asking her spiritual director if she may, in good conscience, refuse this appointment.

Underlying Meaning: No need to look for some hidden, recondite explanation for her 'extreme reaction.' This reaction is well within the normal range. Much as in a family, certain members of a community can 'kill' some other members with their coldness, silence and especially their studied disregard. Note that this can almost always be a misinterpretation of the dreaded person's actions or omissions. At the same time one cannot be constrained personally to expose herself to such an individual on the basis of this possibility.

Suggestions On What To Do: You might suggest that if she can talk to her superior she tell her why such an appointment threatens her personal integrity. She might be wise to put it under strict confidence, in writing. This would give her the opportunity of choosing her words most carefully so as to say just exactly what she wanted to say. If she cannot talk to her superior she would be justified in informing her that 'in conscience' she is unable to accept this assignment.

42. Dialogue

Difficulties Presented: [middle-aged, woman religious] When she was a little girl, this woman said, she used to converse with God. Sometimes she spoke aloud, sometimes her words would not have been audible to another. God's words were never audible, but they were as clear as her own that were not audible. She was very hurt by some of her family and friends to whom she revealed this. They taunted her with remarks such as, "What's this holier than thou stuff? So God talks directly to you! What are you—a saint?" Although she still dialogues with God, at times she feels very ill at ease and even doubts whether she should be doing this. In fact, she is tempted to ask herself whether she could be a phony in continuing these dialogues.

Underlying Meaning: On the face of it this could be self-deception or deliberate deception of others, including a spiritual director. It could also be authentic. With the passing of time everything I heard and saw in this woman tended to confirm the genuine nature of these dialogues, though I do not claim to understand them entirely.

Suggestions On What To Do: Should you encounter this type of person, as you listen to your own 'vibes' you get a sense of whether such a person is authentic. If you do not feel she(he) is genuine, what ought you to do? Tell her that since you are not comfortable dealing with her conversing with God, you should not be her spiritual director. Should you increasingly sense that she is for real, you might encourage her to ask God to tell her what your role as her spiritual director ought to be.

43. Discouragement

Difficulties Presented: [older priest] This man during an eight day retreat said he was terribly discouraged. As he explained it, just about everything he had tried to do for God during his priestly life had ended in failure. He was at the point, he said, where he hesitated to undertake anything because sooner or later he'd "make a botch of it." And he wanted so badly to do something worthwhile for God. He had the need to talk on and on and did so, but never clarified exactly what had motivated him in all the things he had tried to do "for God."

Underlying Meaning: This urge to do something worthwhile for God could have been based simply on a misconception of apostolic success. It could have been a manifestation of a deep-seated need to prove himself by recognized achievement. Thus, personal inadequacy could have been motivating him. It could have been nothing more than a self-recognized utter lack of competency experienced by him as most frustrating.

Suggestions On What To Do: With sufficient time you could sound such a person out by discussing with him(her) his concept of success. You might even begin to feel your way in doing a bit of adult education. You could tell this person, for instance, the following. When one falls short of one's goal, there is an experience of failure, and repetition of such experiences ordinarily results in discouragement. While one must set goals in order to strive for success, he is never sure that a given goal, which is thus set for doing God's work, is in reality God's goal. So it is always and only a working goal. No more than that. God's goal might actually call for him to fall on his face during the quest for his working goal. If one does his best to achieve his working goal and fails, he can feel keenly disappointed, frustrated and perhaps angry. But he has no grounds for losing heart and giving in to discouragement. He has failed only in accomplishing the goals he, or others, established. He has not failed where it really counts, namely, in pursuing God's goals. If the discouraged person seems unable or unwilling to listen to such explanation, it is best perhaps to drop it entirely and later, if and when the opportunity presents itself, to refer him.

44. Dislike

Difficulties Presented: [middle-aged priest] This dignified, reserved, highly intelligent man remarked that he has a deep dislike for a fellow priest. He finds the latter coarse, loud, imprudent and annoying. These feelings bother him in his prayer life. Even though he tells himself that he has not been commanded to like the other person but just to love him, he recognizes that such a distinction is a bit facile. As he sees it, he disapproves of the other man as a person. Perhaps he even resents him as a person. How, he asks, is he to reconcile such attitudes and feelings for this man with his obligation to love him?

Underlying Meaning: There is the possibility that this other man is perceived by him, below the conscious level, as a threat. That might be suspected to be the case were the other man highly regarded or honored within or outside the community. It seems more likely, however, that this other man is the living embodiment of all the personality characteristics he has learned to disapprove of and dislike. That would be enough to explain his reactions. To date, I see no reason to suspect the pathological here.

Suggestions On What To Do: You might suggest to such a person that in prayer he(she) ask Our Lord to let him see this other person through His eyes. Perhaps he will be given the grace of seeing something of what Our Lord finds lovable in this man. But should you get some indication that the priest might need this disparaging perception for his own psychological protection that would change the picture. This dislike could conceivably be displaced from someone this disliked man somehow resembles. This would be a person this priest could not psychologically afford to recognize he really dislikes. At any rate, I think you would wisely refrain from trying to help him cope with his disapproval of this other man. You might have to recognize you could not help him in this specific area. If you felt it necessary, I think it very unlikely that you could find convincing grounds for referring this person for professional help. Nevertheless, you would do well to remain alert for any such opportunity.

45. Doubt

Difficulties Presented: [middle-aged, married man] In the course of a retreat he remarked that his only real problem in life is that he has no peace. He said he knows why. It is because he is continually off balance in terms of doing God's will. He summed it up, "There's always a doubt. You constantly worry that you are doing God's will. Right?"

Underlying Meaning: He struck me as a conscientious, intelligent man. It appeared most unlikely that all he needed was a bit of adult education. In fact, he showed almost immediately that he could not listen to even a suggestion of explanation. At that time of life he should long since have cleared up this whole matter. My clinical impression was that there was something pathological present here. This might be, for instance, a form of camouflaged self-punishment, or else masochistic (gaining gratification from suffering pain and humiliation), or some other psychologically unhealthy incentive.

Suggestions On What To Do: You might feel your way in endeavoring to enlighten such a person. For instance you might say to him(her), "I don't *have* to be right and you don't *have* to be right. You just have to *try* to be right. If you were to die tonight and face God and be able to say to Him, 'I see now that I was wrong but I tried to find out what Your will was and do it,' God would say, 'Come good and faithful servant. I am pleased.' " If he fights that or simply does not hear it, you have an indication that there is a problem here that needs professional help. You could continue directing this person and when the time is right also refer him for professional assistance.

46. Earned

Difficulties Presented: [young single woman] She remarked she has been told innumerable times that God loves her and has tried to believe that, but in vain. There is nothing admirable or in the least lovable about her, she insists. "I have done nothing really worthwhile or good in my life, so how could He love me?" In a strange kind of intellectual way she said she can sort of agree that God loves everyone. But that really doesn't mean anything to her in the sense of having anything to do with her life.

She adds that if she could believe in a really meaningful way that God did love her she couldn't handle the joy.

Underlying Meaning: My impression is that one with this type of problem will seldom be helped by any explanation. The implication that love must be earned usually indicates the aftermath of deeply hurtful learning patterns in early life. The assumption is that during those early years she did not experience real love, but only rewards for good behavior. Moreover it is likely, even though she has made no mention of it, that she regards herself as not only unloved but also as unlovable.

Suggestions On What To Do: After you have heard her(him) out you might remind her that authentic love cannot be earned. Love is never an indebtedness needing to be paid. If she dismisses such considerations or is just not interested in them, you recognize it's not simply a matter of misunderstanding. So spare her further reasoning, clarification, etc. Anticipate that any expression of God's (or anyone else's) 'love' which she feels that she has earned will be tied to great frustration. Why? Because the very fact that it is *earned* gives it the feeling of sticking in her throat. Even though she will have no understanding of it the hunger is for love, not reward. Reward is counterfeit love. It cannot be swallowed and taken within so as to nourish her as a person. If she appears unable to accept love as such, what do you do? Explain, "I am not comfortable in trying to help you experience God's love. While you are seeing me for spiritual direction would you consider also getting such help from someone professionally trained in these matters?"

47. Fantasy

Difficulties Presented: [middle-aged, single woman] This woman remarked that God has gifted her with a vivid, rich imagination. Over a course of many years, she added, she has enjoyed erotic fantasy with a live, male body. This is not the body of someone she knows, but of one she has created in her mind. She said that everything imaginable has happened in this relationship and she has found it sensually most enjoyable. Without anyone suspecting it, this can happen anywhere at any time regardless of whether or not she is alone. Especially if she happens to be reprimanded by her boss or anyone with any kind of authority over her does she move into it immediately. She maintains that she wants to stop this because she knows it is wrong. She has sincerely tried repeatedly, although without notable success. Yet she has never confessed it for two reasons. She didn't know how to say it to a priest, and she couldn't promise God to stop. Her problem, she explains, is that because she knows this is displeasing to God, it interferes with her prayer life.

Underlying Meaning: If she were to ask herself why she continues this behavioral pattern she would in all likelihood say, "Because of the sexual pleasure it gives," and feel that her answer was quite adequate. I would seriously question the correctness of her answer. My position is that whenever a good person wants to terminate behaviors productive of illicit sexual pleasure and repeatedly fails to do so, the pleasure itself is never the *only* explaining factor for the failures. It is not even the *main* one. Such behaviors are invariably *purposive.* Though the person does not even suspect it, there is some need within that person that is thereby being gratified or pacified. Without her recognition a psychological need of the person is thus being satisfied. This will be clearer from some of the actual examples to follow later in this book.

Suggestions On What To Do: To focus attention on the sexual behavior itself would be the last thing to do. If her(his) habitual pattern had happened to be cutting people to ribbons with her tongue, you would not concern yourself, hopefully, with her detailed tongue movements, exact words or tone of voice, but rather try to help her discover *why* she was doing it. What need within her was being satisfied by this behavior of which she disapproved? This woman already knew her behavior was wrong. She had no idea, however, that it was serving any hidden purpose within her, let alone trying to discover which purpose it was taking care of. Even a professional person, presumably, would not know immediately what purpose was being satisfied by such behavior. One thing seen immediately in this woman is that it was functioning in a compensatory role. Pleasure counteracts hurt. She was aware that it spontaneously happened when she was hurt by one in authority. Why did authority enter into it? Incidentally, my suspicion is that it is also much more complex than that. With extra prayer and most attentive listening, you may get some notion what would be going on here. She may unwittingly mention it. Later examples in these pages will give you some further clarification on the *kind* of factors you could be looking for. When a person *sees* and *accepts* the meaning of her behavior—vs. having it *thrust on* her—it can be very beneficial. Should you feel that helping her with this deeper aspect of her problem is beyond you, don't hesitate to tell her so. Her knowledge that you will be with her while she looks also for professional help should prove very supportive.

48. Fantasy

Difficulties Presented: [middle-aged, single woman] For a long time this woman said, she has admired and been very fond of a most admirable married man. Neither he nor his gracious wife has any suspicion, she says, of what is going on. Yet she regularly vividly imagines herself relating warmly and affectionately with him. Initially there is never anything sexual in these fantasies, but as she moves affectionately closer there is arousal on her part which almost always moves into the openly erotic. She holds she is not hurting anyone yet she feels guilty about this.

Underlying Meaning: This is not primarily a problem of fantasy or a sexual problem. Her problem rather is in attempting to sustain a relationship not in keeping with his state in life. She really has not entirely given this man up to his wife, the only one who has the right to that kind of relationship to him. Irrespective of what she has done externally, internally she is still illicitly holding on to him.

Suggestions On What To Do: Realize that by herself(himself) she may not have the strength to make this complete renunciation. When you discern the time to be right, direct her attention to the underlying meaning of her problem. Offer to pray with her after you indicate that only with God's help can she hope to give him up. Show her that she first needs to ask God for the grace to be open to what He wants of her and to give her the strength required for it. In terms of how to go about it, explain to her that fighting it or struggling with it simply is to concentrate on it. It is far better to distract herself by letting her imagination run wild in safe areas, e.g., she might make herself president of the U.S. and begin to clean up the whole White House establishment, etc. She might benefit considerably from a TRUSTED LISTENER (cf. Author's Foreword) while continuing with you in spiritual direction.

49. Fantasy

Difficulties Presented: [middle-aged, single woman] This woman said that she was not ready to make the retreat she was beginning. After three days she came to explain why. She hadn't made a good confession for a long time. She still didn't think she could. She was afraid, she said, to mention sexual fantasy. How could she tell this to a man, especially if he asked for details? These fantasies had not been constant, had been always with the same imagined man, and occurred especially near her period.

Underlying Meaning: The underlying meaning of these fantasies, if any, besides the understandable experiences of arousal associated with menstrual changes in her body chemistry, had not yet surfaced. What was apparent was this woman's need to be freed from the fear of making a good confession.

Suggestions On What To Do: As soon as you, her spiritual director, whether a priest or not, pick up on this kind of problem, you can help prepare this person on *HOW* to go to confession. You may say to her, "Tell the priest, 'Father, I have entertained erotic fantasy a number of times and I suppose about the only thing that never transpired sometime or other was what I never happened to think of.' And that's all. If the confessor should ask for details tell him that you were told that what you said is all you need to say."

50. Fantasy

Difficulties Presented: [middle-aged, married woman] This good woman said she was living in torture. The source of her sufferings, she explained, was her fantasy. In her fantasy she relates frequently in a very warm, affectionate manner to a wonderful man whom she admires and is very fond of. These fantasies usually progress to the unmistakably erotic. This man has never touched her and she feels sure he would be utterly astonished to learn of these fantasies. What makes her feel doubly guilty is the clear recognition that she has a fine husband. She knows he has never in any way cheated on her. Yet he seems completely unaware of the depth of her needs for affection, intimacy and sexual fulfillment. When she hungers for closeness, intimacy and sexual intercourse, he goes to sleep, walks away or otherwise removes himself from her. The strain on her whole nervous system, she added, has been frightful. There is no doubt whatever in her mind that this temptation is from the evil spirit. Moreover, since she has tried everything to fight against the temptation without success, she concludes that the evil spirit is laughing at her.

Underlying Meaning: Below her level of awareness is a sense of experiencing real injustice. This woman did not choose to live the life of a nun. In fact, she gave up intimate sexual relating to every other man in the world for this man and now, at least, he denies it to her. This is an injustice. It is wrong. The psyche being very protective of the person has, quite unknown to her, found in her fantasy a substitute solution for her needed intimacy and sexual intercourse. The injustice of the situation is sufficient to explain the emergence of a personally unacceptable solution without having to attribute it directly to the evil spirit.

Suggestions On What To Do: You might explain to her(him) how the psyche, being protective, would be expected to come up with some such 'solution.' Her sense that this is not a morally acceptable response for her is right on. Later she may recognize that it is a spurious solution. Yet it is an understandable one. The root of her problem is her husband's present non-acceptance of her as wife and lover, which she does not understand. Tell her you do not understand it either. But assure her, should it be called for, that it is highly unlikely that he is using this conduct as a means of expressing his personal rejection of her. What then? The assumption is that he is wrestling with a personal problem. Does she think he could feel threatened by shared intimacy with her? If so, why? Has he been hurt? If so, has she any inkling what that hurt is? Does she have the slightest hunch what might account for his behavior? These points she would do well to explore. Meanwhile she should recognize that her fantasy problem is not primarily a sexual one. Rather it is an interpersonal one. With God's grace what is she to do? In the words from the musical 'South Pacific,' she's "Got to wash that man right out of her hair." She has let that other man fill in where only her husband has the right to be. She has to give him up. And that she will be able to do only with God's grace. Meanwhile she will also ask for special grace to help her husband regain his rightful role as lover, companion and friend. If she can find a TRUSTED LISTENER (cf. Author's Foreword) it could be very helpful to her.

51. Fantasy

Difficulties Presented: [middle-aged, woman religious] While I was directing this woman in a retreat, she spoke repeatedly of herself as the bride, the spouse of Christ. In describing the deep, warm relationship she had developed with her Spouse, she said that it was very intimate and she wanted me to know that, at times, sexual desires had been awakened and in fantasy she had engaged in love play and intercourse with her Spouse. Since He was her Spouse, her husband, she said she saw nothing whatever improper about relating to Christ in these ways. She added that she originally had had some misgivings about this and so had enrolled in a class on spirituality for women religious at a Catholic university. There, according to her report, they were taught that in intimately relating to women, Christ can and does at times touch women religious sexually so as to rouse them even completely. Since He, their Spouse, is God could He not do whatever He wishes, as He wishes? And if He chooses to express His individual personal love in these ways, why is He not free to do so? Besides, would He not make all things He touched pure?

Underlying Meaning: I suspect the faculty member in the Catholic university who gave this course might be very surprised to hear what some thought was being taught in that class. [Besides, were such a relationship of Christ with women religious verified one wonders whether there would be an outcry of male celibates on the score of sex discrimination!] At any rate, the New Testament speaks of the *Church* as the bride of Christ. However, each of a number of women mystics refers to herself as the bride of Christ. All of the latter would, I think, be most surprised if not appalled at this woman's understanding of herself as Christ's wife. In my experience this kind of misconception has done a certain amount of harm to some good women religious. Among other considerations they have rationalized taking back much of that which they surrendered to God under their vow of chastity. They have, as well, presumably in good faith, made it very difficult for Jesus Christ to deal directly with them. The reason is clear. They tend to give anything He might do for them a romantic interpretation.

Suggestions On What To Do: Inasmuch as you would not normally anticipate such a pattern in a mature, well-balanced woman, you may tend to look for indications of other difficulties in such a woman. And very likely you will find some. Even though you do your best not to enter into this whole fantasy area, you will probably be pressed by one of them for a confirmation of what she is doing. You would wisely refrain from in any way giving a confirmation of this unhealthy manner of psychological and spiritual relating. Should she insist on continuing with this relationship to her Spouse, tell her that *in conscience* you may not continue to be her spiritual director.

52. Fantasy

Difficulties Presented: [older single woman] The priest she had for many years as a spiritual director, she almost worshiped. He has been dead for some time. She remarked that he never touched her and was the perfect priest in her eyes. She loves him very much, she added, and as his 'spiritual wife' in fantasy lovingly caresses him, etc. When she dies, she explained, she will be in a spiritual marriage with him. She readily acknowledged that, at times, in loving him she is wholly aroused sexually. This she views as in no way wrong, and explained it thus, "This is because my spiritual love for him is still in the body." She was not open even to consider questioning this whole pattern.

Underlying Meaning: The person with this kind of pattern poses a problem. While claiming she loves this celibate man, in relating affectionately and erotically to him in fantasy, she is, in effect, violating his state of life. A mature woman would see through this at once. She would also know that a spiritual director would immediately spot something wrong in such a pattern. The fact that this woman freely acknowledged such a relationship while justifying it, bespeaks in her some lack of maturity.

Suggestions On What To Do: You will soon sense whether a person with such experiences is open to any indication that this might be unacceptable. If so, you might ask her(him) if there is anyone in the area whom she considers really qualified in spirituality. If she names someone, inquire if she would be willing to ask this person whether or not her fantasy experiences are wholly permissible. On the assumption that she is unable to name someone, you could ask her if she would be willing to present this to two or three different confessors she respects, and get their judgments. If she wants to know why you are making this request of her, tell her you are not comfortable with this matter. If you are unable to get her to question her behavior on any score, inform her that you are too uncomfortable with this relationship of hers to be her spiritual director.

53. Fear

Difficulties Presented: [young married man] His problem, he stated, is he just can't get close to Christ, "Because He's a stranger." He explained he is deathly afraid of getting close to anyone he respects, and is forced to give that person a wide berth. Yet he is not a socially timid man in all situations. In fact, he noted, he has no problem whatever in walking into any lower class bar or tavern and meeting anyone there. "Actually," he said, "I feel comfortable with prostitutes and other social derelicts, though my wife would object strenuously if she knew; yet I'm really at home with them." In terms of spiritual growth, he asked, "How can I be expected to relate closely to and pray to a perfect stranger?"

Underlying Meaning: This kind of problem seems to flow invariably from a self-concept that was badly damaged early in life. Thereafter the likelihood of someone he looks up to getting close enough to really see what he is like, is a hideous prospect. On the other hand, he can afford to risk letting these other kinds of people in close because in his mind they are no good either, so they can't look down on him.

Suggestions On What To Do: This type of person can readily be precipitated into a state of anxiety by urging or even encouraging him(her) to get closer to Jesus Christ. Such an undertaking is far beyond his present strengths. In fact, he could experience such urging as unbearable pressure, giving rise to self-incrimination, guilt, insecurity, etc. The wiser course here would be to strive not to get trapped in the problem areas of this person. Instead, when the time seems right, suggest he also see someone professionally trained to work with people in the area of human anxieties.

54. Fear

Difficulties Presented: [middle-aged, single woman] During a retreat, this woman said she frequently experiences great fear though she doesn't know of what. She also finds that she is most inconstant in her behavior, especially when she is not on her proper diet. Then she feels listless and her attitude towards the diet and a number of other things she characterized as, "to hell with it." Some time back she had a physical after which she said, her doctor told her she has hypoglycemia. She has discovered, as well, that when she disregards her diet she tends to feel more afraid.

Underlying Meaning: It appeared that much of her problem, at least, stems from chemical imbalance. My impression was that the main source of her problems is medical rather than psychological.

Suggestions On What To Do: It is very seldom threatening or offensive to suggest to such a person that she(he) get a complete physical examination. Urge her to tell her physician that her behavior has been inconstant and that she has experienced some fear. This would lend clarification to your spiritual direction, inasmuch as you would have some medical explanations for her otherwise bewildering behaviors. It would also facilitate the physician's diagnosis. You could well continue with her in spiritual direction. When she reports inconstant behavior, ask whether she is following her diet before looking for other causes.

55. Fear

Difficulties Presented: [young married woman] This woman remarked, during a week-end retreat, that she is unable to pray, to think of God, or even to relax, because she lives in an agony of fear. It is the specific fear that she will kill her baby. It haunts her sleep as well as her waking hours, so that she cannot escape it.

Underlying Meaning: This excruciating type of fear is assumed to have a meanng of which she wouldn't have the slightest suspicion. The psychological presumption is that such a fear is one manifestation of an utterly incredible yet powerful urge within her to hurt of even destroy her baby. It may carry with it the experience of a completely baffling and confusing feeling of guilt. This fear is postulated to be the inclination's only expression, besides the puzzling guilt, that she can psychologically afford to face. She will have not even a suspicion of the abnormal content underlying this urge. In a professional relationship she could gradually become aware of the meaning of this fear. Then with professional help she would search to uncover the source of the underlying hostility. Once that source was identified, with the help of God's grace she could begin to cope with it.

Suggestions On What To Do: You might well point out to her(him) that, as she is aware, her fear does not respond to reason. Hence there must be more to this very real experience than either of you recognizes. You do not feel qualified to deal with such an important feeling area. Accordingly, you would be more comfortable while she is coming to you for spiritual direction if she would consider also seeing one who is trained in such matters to help her with this particular fear.

56. Fear

Difficulties Presented: [young single woman] She stated, during a retreat, that she is forced to be somewhat cold and aloof with even those closest to her. She simply could not afford to be warm and affectionate with anyone. The reason, she explained, is that she is afraid she could not *control* it, even if she gave in just a little bit. For much the same reason, she asserted, she cannot afford ever to feel the least anger. She lives in dread of affection and anger.

Underlying Meaning: She is not a free woman. This fear of losing control of self could have any one of several sources. Because of the way the human psyche works, in all likelihood she has not even a clue to its origin or meaning. This fear of losing control would ordinarily be expected to have come from very early, unhealthy, learning patterns in life. The original happenings would have been automatically blotted out of memory. Their impact, however, is still a dynamic of the person's experience and behavior. What is the source of this twofold fear? It is impossible to listen briefly to such a person and immediately identify it. For instance, this fear could be a manifestation of basic distrust of self, or of personal insecurity or inadequacy. Again it could mask her great fear of personal rejection, her deep dislike of self, or some other well concealed psychological content.

Suggestions On What To Do: Endeavor to understand how delicate this is. When you feel the time is right, suggest to her(him) that while with you she permit herself to feel a bit of affection or anger toward someone she knows. Then watch her reaction. If she is able to accept this suggestion, continue to help her become free to feel these two experiences. If, however, the expected occurs and there appears to be a disproportionate disturbance within her, discontinue. Should she begin to panic, or confess to increased anxiety, these would be caution flags for you. Especially if she indicates clearly a very poor self-concept, assume there is more here than you have been trained to deal with. Then try later to find the opportunity to suggest that she also see someone trained in these two areas of feelings of affection and anger, while you help her with spiritual direction.

57. Fear

Difficulties Presented: [young single woman] She explained, during a retreat, that she relates to God as Beauty, Power, and Majesty. In the New Testament she reads only St. Paul. She does not mind reading *about* Jesus as long as she does not have to relate *to* him. There is no way, she insists, that she could get near him personally. She is unable to say why, but knows that even the thought of it chills her. The one thing she is sure of is that she could not trust him. Meanwhile she is happy to relate to God in an impersonal way, particularly in nature.

Underlying Meaning: As I listened, day after day, I recognized that this distaste or fear was generalized to men. As I had suspected, she indicated she had been painfully taught earlier in life that men are not to be trusted. So she cannot afford to get close to the man Christ. These are things she told me without herself being aware of saying them or even recognizing them as an underlying explanation.

Suggestions On What To Do: You might refer a woman with this type of problem for professional help and given the right clinical person, it could prove beneficial. You might be inclined to explain to her that this problem had arisen from her generalizing her experience with one or more untrustworthy men to all men. This would most likely be of no benefit. Indeed it could be harmful. The injury is not to her reasoning faculty so explanations do not touch it. A woman with this type of difficulty, seeking a spiritual director, can be predicted to seek out another woman. If you are that woman spiritual director, what is the best way for you to help her? In my judgment it is this: if you can find a gentle, patient, and completely trustworthy male spiritual director, urge her to ask him to be her spiritual director. Tell her you are doing this in conscience because you really care about her. Assure her you will be glad if she would come to see you from time to time to visit, but not for spiritual direction. Starting to trust him may take many months, but little by little as she talks with him she will be less uncomfortable when close to Christ in prayer. She will find less difficulty in beginning to read the gospels, and start to feel freed as a woman. At all costs the man spiritual director should avoid asking her to trust him. This could be most threatening to her. He should wait patiently for her to give the first signs of a blossoming trust. This she may do only after many months of testing.

58. Fear

Difficulties Presented: [young single woman] During a retreat in which I was her director this young woman confided that she was tortured by the fear that she would "lose her mind." She felt that she was already well into the process of "going crazy."

Underlying Meaning: While this might conceivably have been a play for attention or compassion, the only safe assumption I felt I could make was that she was deeply disturbed psychologically.

Suggestions On What To Do: I would advise strongly against supplying such a person with any grounds for thinking that particular prayers or any specific spiritual practice would be the route to healing. You would not in any way discourage her(him) from praying, receiving the sacraments, etc. It would seem very unwise, however, to encourage her to anticipate cures from such means. You would do well to refer her for professional help as early as possible. If you could manage to refer her during the first session on the score that you do not feel qualified to help her with such a fear, any rejection she would experience from this referral should not be intense. The reason it should not be intense is that she had not yet let you really get to know her. If you would prefer to continue with her in spiritual direction, do so. Meanwhile make sure not to be trapped by her in concentrating on these her fears of developing full-blown mental illness.

59. Fear

Difficulties Presented: [middle-aged, single woman] As she spoke at some length, during a retreat, this woman kept returning to the same point. She had a persistent feeling of fear that God wants her either to do something very difficult or to discontinue something she is presently doing and does not want to stop. She can not tell which. This leaves her in a state of inner turbulence, making it difficult for her to relax, to sleep, to be at peace.

Underlying Meaning: Be wary of the assumption that every retreatant should increasingly feel deeply at peace as the retreat progresses. This kind of fear indicates a psychological happening below the level of her awareness which may or may not be from God. It does, however, need to be surfaced in her consciousness and resolved, so that she may live in peace.

Suggestions On What To Do: You might find a time when the two of you could have a session that, if needed, could go over two hours. You might tell her(him) that as yet you do not know the meaning of her inner commotion, but, if she wished, she might come in and talk about it at length. Your role would be to listen most closely. Then little by little, through the discernment of spirits, one of you would most likely be able to recognize whether or not these feelings were from God. It could be, for example, that clearly God is asking her for complete surrender to His will, which might terrify her. Or He could be asking her to give up someone or something illicit that she is most reluctant to part with. She would most likely at least confirm your finding, if indeed she does not herself identify what is troubling her. Then she could take whatever steps seemed necessary to bring her peace. If this is not being resolved in spiritual direction, a TRUSTED LISTENER (cf. Author's Foreword) could be of real help.

60. Fear

Difficulties Presented: [young single woman] This young woman remarked that she lives in the fear that she will end up like one of the old, dried up, gossipy, character-assassinating, lonely, females she has known. (A young man reported a similar fear of becoming one of the old men who are bitter, lonely and disillusioned. "How," he asked, "can I keep my late years from becoming that?")

Underlying Meaning: Is there more here than appears, or is this simply a readily understandable dread of winding up in one's life as a human disaster? It is necessary to feel one's way in judging the nature of this type of fear. One clue would be the intensity of the feeling of fear. A haunting, obsessing fear could lead you to suspect there is more than is visible here. For instance, it might be that all unknowingly a deeply seated terror was being displaced onto the handy target of a dismaying projection of one's old age. If, however, the fear seemed to be but a reasonable emotional response to a possible future calamitous, personal happening there would be no reason to suspect the presence of the pathological.

Suggestions On What To Do: You might first discuss with her(him) the tragedy of such eventualities in the lives of women and men. Then point out that these elderly people did not suddenly develop such unacceptable behavior. Moreover, you could give her the assurance that she cannot be helplessly forced into such a role in the last years of her life. Then closely observe the reaction. If she sees this, agrees and feels relieved then the problem is beginning to be resolved. If, however, she is unable to hear such a presentation or if it makes no impact whatever on her fear, then what? It would be well to conclude that this calls for professional help and so you look for an opportunity to refer. You might tell her you do not feel qualified to help in this fear experience. Then ask if it would be possible for her to see one educated to deal with such emotions, while she continues in spiritual direction with you.

61. Fear

Difficulties Presented: [middle-aged, woman religious] This woman came during a retreat and said immediately that she was miserable. She stated that she had never wanted to be a religious. The reason she entered the convent was because of her conviction that God wanted her to be a nun. Constantly she feels as though there is something deep inside her being suffocated. Her statement was that although she doesn't understand it she knows that to be in religious life means violating herself as a person. She remarked, "My vocation was based on fear—fear of God. I remain in religion solely out of fear of Him."

Underlying Meaning: There are many things in life that we do not like to do. We ought never let this be a basis for our choices. It is important to recognize that there are people who not only do not *like* to be in religious life (or in a marriage, etc.,) but also do not *choose* to be there. They remain there only out of fear. Where that is the case, until it is resolved one way or the other, the person experiences enslavement and deep, ongoing frustration. This is not really a free choice of a state of life. Rather it is a *yielding* to a state of life out of fear of doing otherwise.

Suggestions On What To Do: I think that you need to take the responsibility, since this person is unable to, for telling such a person that she(he) should begin a process of prayerful discernment. She is to begin by regarding herself *free* to seek the state of life God *wants* her in and the state of life in which *she wants* to serve Him. Fear, even of God, is not the proper motivation for the choice of a state of life. God does not want slavery. He wants a service from love. Given these circumstances, her most pressing question will be: In what state of life does she want to live for God? She needs to understand this.

62. Fear

Difficulties Presented: [middle-aged, married man] This man, a teacher, said he feels constantly afraid. He wakes up in the morning afraid, although he is not certain what he fears. He has been teaching for years, yet feels fear every time he walks into a class. He has asked himself what he fears in there. His answer is, "The students might mutiny against me, or some one student defy my authority, or so many threatening things could take place there. Yet even if I had a guarantee that absolutely nothing whatever of a threatening nature could happen, I am sure that I would still feel afraid. Why, I don't know."

Underlying Meaning: This man is manifesting an almost classic example of pathological anxiety. The assumption here is that the psychological disturbance underlying these fears calls for professional help. The source of such fears would have been in his early life, of which he almost certainly has no recall here and now.

Suggestions On What To Do: Endeavoring to show this man that his fears are largely groundless would be a futile effort. Moreover doing so would very likely jeopardize your relationship with him(her). No matter what his head might say, in his stomach he continues to experience the grip of fear. The decision to continue with him in spiritual direction needs your clear recognition that this is not a free man. He is preoccupied with the emotions produced by continually experienced threats, even though he is unable to identify the dangers which threaten him. Lacking this recognition that he is preoccupied with these fears, you would also, unwittingly, be courting great frustration. My advice would be to refer him, at the earliest opportunity, while continuing as his director.

63. Feelings

Difficulties Presented: [young single woman] After indicating some of the wrong things she has done and is still doing this woman stressed one point. That point is that right up to the present moment she has never experienced *feelings* of guilt or sorrow for any of her wrongs. To her surprise she is nevertheless sorry for those she has hurt. The possibility that she should give a certain person up has occurred to her in passing, but she just is not sure about this. Meanwhile she is eager for spiritual direction.

Underlying Meaning: As became clear to her later on, her last defense against having to change her behavior was her not *feeling* guilt or sorrow. In time, feelings of guilt and sorrow surfaced. Then there came a day when she remarked that she could not live with these feelings, and knew she had to alter her behavior. Once she determined to change, with God's help, she began to experience deep peace.

Suggestions On What To Do: Without your saying a word in moral judgment, especially if you are a priest or religious, a person with some such pattern knows exactly where you stand. That is, there is no need for you to spell out your position in terms of the rightness or wrongness of her(his) behavior. At least early in the relationship you would do well to carefully avoid the inclination to make clear where the Church stands on these reported behaviors. What if you should yield to this inclination before she directly or indirectly asks you? It could have the effect of postponing almost indefinitely her being able to *see* what she must do. Meanwhile, I think the wisest course for you is to *listen* to her and wait for the Holy Spirit to guide her.

64. Frightened

Difficulties Presented: [middle-aged, woman religious] She wrote: "I'm frightened, very frightened. Maybe I'm making a mountain out of a molehill, but telling you about it can't make things worse. If Satan is just having a ball at my expense, it won't do any harm to expose him. If, on the other hand, this is all my own doing, it will still help just to tell you about it. I don't know how to say this. I'm not trying to be melodramatic. I'm not 'hearing voices,' but it's almost equivalent to that. Unwanted thoughts come into my mind regarding faith and hope. They come *fast* as if someone else were saying these things to me. I think I'm sane! For example, I've been in the habit of making acts of love when I awaken at night. Recently when I try to do that, the thought comes quick as a flash, 'There is no God' or 'Why bother? You don't really love Him.' There is always a deep yearning to receive the Eucharist, but at the moment I receive the Host, 'This isn't Jesus; it's just plain bread.' Today I tried to pray acts of faith, hope, love and contrition, in spite of my general inability to really pray. I felt as if I were being sneered at: 'Hypocrite, you're just mouthing words. You no longer really believe in Him; how can you make an act of faith? How can you hope? What is there to hope for? Whom are you loving? There's nobody there.'

"When I recall last year's joyful experiences, I hear, 'You still believe that? You just had yourself psyched up.' At those times I am reassured by the memory of your telling me that they *were* for real. At least I still have faith in you. When I decided to write you about this, I heard 'Don't do that. He'll just think you're very silly. Besides, you should be more considerate of him; he already has his hands full. Don't bother anybody with these foolish thoughts.' All of this is accompanied with deep depression and discouragement. Deep down I know I believe in God and I think I love Him though I feel nothing.

"This morning, in desperation, I pleaded with Him to help me in some way. I closed my Bible and opened it completely at random. The place where it fell open was at St. Luke's account of Satan tempting Jesus. The desolation remained, but I began to wonder whether He was permitting Satan to test me to increase my realization of how very much I need Him.

"If this is the price which must be paid to be united to Him in His own time, it's what I want, too. I simply get really scared."

Underlying Meaning: There is always the possibility in this type of situation that something wholly below the conscious level is struggling against such a person's getting close to God. Let us assume that an example of the kind of thing I am referring to might be helpful here. Could it be that she had unknowingly come to identify her father who had rejected her with God her Father? In that context some of what she had reported would make sense. Aside from some such possibility, you see immediately that her report fits the role of the evil spirit admirably. She is left very frightened. Her faith and hope are being attacked. There is the denial of God's existence and the asserting of the futility of her even trying. She is told she does not love Him. The real presence is denied. As a person she is put down. Each time that she reaches out in hope she is dashed down. Finally there is the strong, repeated urging that she not tell anybody about any of this. She receives a confirmation that this is from the enemy by opening the Bible at random and reading. God can and does communicate to certain people in this way.

Suggestions On What To Do: With a person reporting this kind of experience, listen to see if something pathological is being indicated. If so, you should be able to catch enough of it to know whether it calls for referral, even though you do not understand it. Otherwise reinforce her(his) faith, her hope and her love for God. Confirm her as a person. Reassure her on the specific things that frighten her. Assure her of your availability. Tell her frankly that though you don't understand fully what is going on here, you know that she is safe in God's love. After you have asked the guidance of the Holy Spirit say whatever else you think you should say to her.

65. Frustrated

Difficulties Presented: [middle-aged, woman religious] A few days after she came for her annual 8 day directed retreat, this pleasant woman told me that the affliction of her life was that she had not received the Sacrament of Reconciliation for years. It was her consuming desire to do so but as often as she had tried, she had not succeeded. She just could not force herself to go. Every year at her retreat, she said, she told herself that this year she would make it, but she never did. She declared that from experience she knew without a doubt that once again she was destined to return home without having received the sacrament. What puzzled her was that she did not have even an inkling why she had this problem. Her life was one of frustration, confusion, guilt, and deep discouragement.

Underlying Meaning: There was nothing spurious or simulated in her claim that she had no notion of why. That is usual in this type of difficulty. As this woman talked on, day after day, she told me how close she had been to her mother, until her mother had been taken from her very suddenly. Mentally and emotionally this paralyzed her. Later she had gone for a rather routine biopsy because of a small lump on her breast, and in utter shock awakened to find she had had a radical mastectomy. She confided that it had horribly disfigured her as a woman and as a person. And yet, she assured me, she had through all these years generously and faithfully served God. Then she got the first inkling that she was holding God responsible for her mother being so abruptly snatched from her and for her own disfigurement. She saw that although she had never so much as suspected it, she was still very angry at God. How could she ask forgiveness from One who had thus let her down after she had served Him so well? Once she recognized this, she could understand that she needed the great grace to be able to forgive God first before she could go to Him and ask His forgiveness. With His grace, she did so, was able to receive the sacrament and had complete peace. From a sole theological perspective this might look doctrinally doubtful. From a psychological one this was a needed preliminary to her further spiritual growth.

Suggestions On What To Do: The person with this type of suffering seems to me to need your *compassionate* listening. Time does not do a great deal to lessen this kind of hurt, so the sufferer must directly cope with it. It seems that such a person has the grace to cope but God wishes her (him) not to do it alone. With such a person you may find yourself groping about for an explanation of what is going on. What you do know is that she is really *hurting*. Perhaps that is all you need to know, and that when you compassionate with this person, God's grace will do the rest.

66. Guilt

Difficulties Presented: [middle-aged, married woman] This sensible woman reported that she carries daily a tremendous burden of guilt which she does not feel free to share even with her husband. She is certain that this guilt stems in its entirety from her one horrifying experience, as a little child, of having a strange man sexually expose himself to her.

Underlying Meaning: Psychological theoreticians are not in full accord in explaining the guilt resulting from such experiences. Unfortunately this is not a terribly uncommon kind of response, and it has caused much suffering. No one seems certain why the simple witnessing of such adult behavior by a little girl child should cause an experience of guilt in her which would continue to afflict her into womanhood. At any rate it is never simply a matter of a lack of the understanding of personal imputability.

Suggestions On What To Do: You are safe in explaining to such a woman that as long as God allows her to carry this cross, He will give her sufficient strength to do so. Later if there should be promising professional help available you could prudently see if there might be an occasion to refer her. Your ongoing spiritual direction, which ought to try to skirt the matter of the guilt as much as possible, can be beneficial spiritually to such a person. You could inform her that she is free to ask God to remove this affliction from her, which He will do if He sees that's best for her. At the same time she ought to leave God free to love her the way He wants.

67. Guilt

Difficulties Presented: [middle-aged, single woman] When she was only five years of age, this woman reported, she was sexually molested by a man. Though she did not understand what was happening, her mother had happened onto the scene and screamed in a way that went right through her. She had tried repeatedly to talk to her father about it but he invariably dusted her off and did not care to talk about what had happened. She was afraid to ask her mother. She felt *very guilty*. When as a teenager she finally realized what the man had done to her, she was infuriated. She still feels angry but also guilty. At one time, she added, she was going steady with a nice young man but could not even consider the remote possibility of sexual relations. Very motherly, she relates readily with little children, understands them and is perceptive of their needs, sensitivities, reactions, etc. She does not let any man really close to her. In fact, she permits no one to get very near her, even though a few people feel they truly know her. "They just think so. I never let them past a certain point." She talked about a prayerful contemplation she had of washing Christ's feet. "Our Lord asked me, 'You can't look at me?' And I couldn't. I knew this had to do with that original terrible experience."

Underlying Meaning: It is still not clear why a woman would feel guilt subsequent to being molested early in her life. To a man this would not make sense. Yet a number of these women do experience lasting guilt. In this woman some of the guilt would appear to have originated in her perception of the strange behavior of her parents. They would not talk to her about it so, she concluded, it must have been her fault. And the way her mother especially reacted, it must have been an unpardonable thing that she had done.

Suggestions On What To Do: Again you may compassionate this type of person as you listen to her express her agony. You might want to tell her that she is not alone in this kind of experience. Many a woman who as a child was victimized in this manner is unable to explain her guilt feelings which persist. This is a cross He will give her the grace to carry for Him. She may ask Him in prayer to relieve her of this cross, but urge her to leave Him free to love her the way He chooses. There is no reason why such a woman could not benefit from spiritual direction. If and when she talks about this early experience or the subsequent suffering, you would be wise to listen with as little commenting as possible.

68. Guilt

Difficulties Presented: [middle-aged, single woman] This woman remarked that she experiences a great deal of guilt. She feels guilty about her confessions, because it is always the same old story of being uncharitable, etc. She feels guilty sitting down to read the newspaper even at the end of a very hard day when she feels beat. She senses that guilt has kept her real apostolic effectiveness under wraps. She insisted that even though she can't explain it, she knows that she is a coward.

Underlying Meaning: I had no idea what precisely was beneath all these feelings, so I listened over a period of months. She felt better when she was able to admit to me that at times she has had a wish to be in the comforting arms of a wonderful man. She sensed that this wish somehow held the key to understanding more about herself. Finally she realized that she has been terribly afraid all her adult life to let her affectionate nature show through. She has always maintained a cool reserve and a distance from people, especially from certain people, out of fear. This she described as the fear that she couldn't handle the wrong affection some might want from her, or that she might get hurt from being warm to others. She said she now sees that the reason she felt so guilty is clear. She has wanted to serve Christ all her life. Now she faces the naked truth that out of fear she had kept her apostolic clout under wraps for years. No wonder, she said, she knew she was a coward. She had longed to give herself generously to work for Christ's Kingdom and had been paralyzed in inactivity because of this fear.

Suggestions On What To Do: Once such a person has gained these insights you can help her(him) grow spiritually as she regains her psychological health. Even if you should be aware of what is happening within her, until she sees on her own what is going on, your most promising course is attentive listening. You might also judge that in addition to your helping spiritual direction, she could benefit from the assistance of the right professional person.

69. Hearing

Difficulties Presented: [middle-aged single woman] With the passing of the weeks this woman increasingly impressed me as an intelligent, stable person. Her abiding concern rather than worry has been about what she 'hears' from God. She 'hears' specific words, such as, "Come deeply within and be with me." That does not mean to her that she is to leave the world nor withdraw from others. What she is 'hearing' is not vocal. There is no sound. Yet the words are unambiguous and always the same. She said, "I can distract myself and at times I don't want to do what they tell me." Still she is convinced that these are from God and that they tell her what He wants.

Underlying Meaning: Imagination can play tricks on certain good people so that they 'hear', 'see' or 'feel' things that are not really there. Every spiritual director would do well to reflect that kindness is never a justification for misleading a person. If it is nothing but a product of one's imagination, don't pretend otherwise. Notwithstanding, neither this realization nor a psychological frame of explanation which is closed off to the possibility of the supernatural ought to be allowed to blind a spiritual director to what *is*. In short, while some such reported 'experiences' can be merely imagined or misleading, God *can* do such things. At times the indications are that He *is* the author of such experiences. The two extremes are gullibility and incredulousness. Between lies a discerning openness. With this woman I judged that these 'voices' were of God, and the passing of time only reinforced that judgment.

Suggestions On What To Do: You need to be particularly discerning when listening to a person telling about such experiences. Be slow to accept as authentic any such reports. In general it is a wise policy to supplement the discernment of spirits with good common sense. A person reporting such 'hearings' might need gently to be dissuaded by you from accepting her(his) experiences as clearly or even probably from God. On the other hand, she might need your supporting confirmation that this is indeed from God.

70. Homosexuality

Difficulties Presented: [young single man] This man during a retreat said he very much wanted to follow Christ, but was not sure how he could bring this off since he was gay.

Underlying Meaning: It is often difficult when listening to such a person (as also to a bisexual man or woman) to know whether the person is thinking and talking about his gay orientation, and if so, why he sees this as an obstacle, or about his sexual acts. In a word does he see his gay orientation itself as an obstacle to following Christ, or is he trying to see how he can reconcile his gay lifestyle with Christ's discipleship.

Suggestions On What To Do: I regard it as a very perilous risk to advise or encourage a gay person to seek professional help in order to change his(her) sexual orientation. In general I have found that no such change is brought about by professional help. [I recall here a young woman, a lesbian, who years ago was coming to me for professional psychological help. Although we were not dealing with her lesbianism, she said she chose to discontinue the therapy because she became afraid that as she got psychologically stronger she might lose her lesbianism and become a neuter! Such a prospect horrified her.] A man or woman with this sexual pattern may need to be informed that a gay *orientation* carries no morality whatever. There may be the further need to clarify that overt, gay, sexual *actions* are not morally acceptable in the eyes of the Church. It is of the utmost importance that a spiritual director when dealing with a gay person try to appreciate the terribly difficult position this person is in. He(she) has taken no vow of celibacy. Yet in order to keep God's law this one is being asked to lead a life which can be experienced as a violation of his person. You would feel deeply for such a person, even though you don't know this pain from personal experience. This means you are unable to share this suffering. To such a one who is very discouraged it may seem good to stress that with God's grace all things are possible.

71. Hostility

Difficulties Presented: [young single man] This man, a black college student, was popular with other students and liked by the faculty. Things were going well for him, he said, and so he felt he should be content and happy. But while not unhappy, he was always tense. Moreover from time to time, to his utter surprise, he was almost overwhelmed by an unbelievably strong urge to smash or destroy someone. This was directed at white persons, not excluding those white persons he knew and liked. And this frightened him, because, as he put it, "It's so strong I'm not sure I can control it. And I know I could kill whitey with my bare hands."

Underlying Meaning: He was indicating that deeply within him was a rage whose existence, in years gone by, he had not even suspected. When it would erupt it did so with such intensity that he questioned whether he could remain in control. As he continued to talk about it he remarked, "And you know if I did flip out and killed whitey even most painfully, I know I'd feel I still wouldn't be even. He took my manhood, my personhood, and I would have taken only his life." He found these feelings and urges exceedingly difficult to reconcile with his relationship to God. As far as he could tell, this buried rage was the product of his cumulative experience of being accepted 'in his place' by whites. That 'place' seemed vaguely to him to be somewhere between the status of a child and that of a treasured family pet. When he talked about it he was conscious of deep pain and smoldering fury.

Suggestions On What To Do: Even though apprehensive, try to be compassionate with such a one. After listening to him(her) for some time, point out the importance of his having recognized that he needs help in controlling such urges. Tell him that you do not feel professionally qualified to help with these feelings and inclinations, and ask him if while he continues to see you about his spiritual life, he would also get help in handling these strong urges from someone professionally qualified to give such help. If so, tell him you will, if he wishes, inquire about who would be the most qualified professional person in the immediate area.

72. Hurt

Difficulties Presented: [older woman religious] With a professional background in nursing, this woman said that she has the responsibility of the nursing care of all older ill persons in her community. She maintains that she has been hurt by these people almost to the point of its destroying her. She has spent herself in seeing to their every need. Nonetheless some repeatedly have said publicly that they are not being properly looked after and are badly in need of competent care. "And not one nun has spoken up in my defense." It is impossible, she says, for her to describe the hurt, the sense of betrayal, the disloyalty she experiences. Her anger ties her stomach in knots. It will allow her no relaxation. It bothers her to find herself, in her anger, even using language which she feels would shock people if they knew.

Underlying Meaning: A woman religious can be hurt by her own sisters as she normally could not be by those outside the community. [To a lesser degree I have found that this appears true also for men living in religious community.] I think the ingratitude of her religious sisters can hurt a woman deeply, and result in great discouragement. "What's the point of staying in community?" this woman asked. While I see this type of person as not manifesting a strong sense of adequacy and security, I think the presenting problem needs to be addressed and coped with. Here is a woman who sees herself being mistreated by these other women. And regardless of how they see it, that ill-treatment is damaging to this woman.

Suggestions On What To Do: Just to find someone who will really listen, without judging or even questioning helps. Very likely for some time such a person has not had anyone who cares enough to do that. She cannot be rushed. After some time you might help her by drawing a line between unacceptable *behavior* and the *person* from whom this behavior comes. Remind her that God always makes this distinction in dealing with each of us. Point out that such maltreatment is never acceptable and should be resented no matter from whom it would come. Then, help her either (a) forgive each of these persons (done not face to face but in her prayer to God), or (b) leave the judging of their guilt to God. Reassure her that she can in this way continue fruitfully in spiritual direction. A TRUSTED LISTENER (cf. Author's Foreword) might be of considerable help to her.

73. Immaturity

Difficulties Presented: [younger middle-aged priest] Several times, this man says, he has put a question to himself. Why doesn't he have any notable desire to undertake any priestly duties? He is beginning to understand that it is not so much a lack of desire as an apprehension about tackling any adult undertaking. He simply doesn't feel up to it. As he sees it, he wasn't brought up to function that way. He had lived for years under the protective umbrella of his parents. They were the ones who took responsibility for almost everything. From there he went directly to the seminary under the umbrella of the bishop and his other superiors. They took up where his parents had left off. As long as he did what they wanted, he had no personal responsibility for making decisions. His parents and his religious superiors wanted him to become a priest. So that was good enough for him. Now he is having questions about his priesthood also. He is intelligent and says that the priesthood was never his own choice. Yet, to even think about leaving and striking out on his own terrorizes him.

Underlying Meaning: In some ways he feels he is still a boy in a man's body. Psychologically not yet fully an adult, he is aware that most of his companions in the seminary insisted on being their own men. They had nothing of his passive, receptive over-all attitude, but still, on the whole, they were properly obedient. He recognizes this and yet has some understanding of how he grew to be the way he is.

Suggestions On What To Do: This type of individual could benefit considerably from your spiritual direction if he(she) were at the same time to receive professional assistance. He should not be difficult to refer because he has an awareness of his need for help in dealing with his feelings and emotions when contemplating undertaking adult roles. I would think more growth psychologically and spiritually is a requisite for his tackling the problem of his vocation.

74. Inadequacy

Difficulties Presented: [middle-aged priest] As far back as he can remember, this man stated during a 30 day retreat, he has lived in fear. His own self-characterization was, "I'm incapable of loving, because I'm a taker, not a giver, and empty." His life, he disclosed, is best summed up as a record of personal failures. "Yet I've wanted to scream at people, 'It's not my fault. I was dealt a bad hand.' " Under the burden of intense self-loathing and self-hatred he had been very close to despair, "To throwing in the old towel." Only lately had he realized that he is very resentful of God and very angry at Him. It puzzled him to recognize that he accuses God of doing too much and, at the same time, of not doing enough in his life. That he has never forgiven God was a recent, surprising awareness. "Could that be why I haven't been able to let Him near me?" he asked. As a youth, he said he was afraid of just about everything and he just drifted into the priesthood. It seemed the easiest, the least threatening course available. Yet as far back as he can recall he gave up prayer, because he felt it was not suited to him. Now he feels he has to start to do something about it.

Underlying Meaning: The presence of a pervasive, serious personality problem here would be difficult to miss. A spiritual director would sense that, without deep healing, spiritual direction would be insufficient. I think that further reflection would also show that professional help without the equivalent, at least, of spiritual direction would not be enough. Clearly, this man was not ready to begin a 30 day retreat. But he needed help to get started to straighten out his life.

Suggestions On What To Do: At least for the time being, assuming this kind of person to be getting professional help, which would appear to be essential, all I would advise you to do is listen. Say as little as possible. Any other course of action on your part could pose an unnecessary risk of hurting him(her). It might be well to remind yourself that the Holy Spirit is working with you as well as with him. If, however, after prayer you should feel that you ought not have this man in spiritual direction, then gently tell him you do not feel really qualified to help him.

75. Infatuation

Difficulties Presented: [younger middle-aged, single woman] She says there is no way she is able to get that man (not marriageable to her) out of her hair. While she is not sure, she thinks he may have proposed marriage to her once. To be safe she said no. Over and above the consideration that she would not want him to leave his commitments, she remarked, "It wouldn't work for the two of us." She is continually feeling not only hurt but crushed either by what he does or fails to do. What she should do is beyond her.

Underlying Meaning: This woman does not appear to have a strong sense of personal adequacy, or steadfast self-concept. Her head tells her that on at least two scores she should give up this man. She is unable to do so. Her reactions would be expected more in a love-smitten teen-ager. Her acute vulnerability to being crushed says more about her than about this other person. It seems strange that she would not even be certain whether or not he had proposed.

Suggestions On What To Do: Let her(him) talk. It will help her. Be very careful not to let her involve you as a middleman in order to help her clarify this man's intentions, etc. Especially if she maintains that she is helplessly 'in love' with him, look for an early opportunity to refer her for professional assistance.

76. Insecurity

Difficulties Presented: [older priest] While making an 8 day directed retreat this man said that his cross is living with general insecurity. He told of building a number of parish buildings, including a church, and explained that, between us, his main motive in putting up these buildings had been to get recognition and deserved praise. He did get some, but it was not satisfying, because it was just for what he had done and not for him as a person. The latter is what he had sought.

Underlying Meaning: Everyone appreciates praise from the right people. This was something more than that. This man seemed to be revealing a low self-concept. It appeared to be unhealthy.

Suggestions On What To Do: Ask yourself if you sense that such a person would be open to consider the possibility of professional help. In this instance, my own judgment was that the eight day retreat was not the proper time to undertake this referral, unless the retreatant himself would open the conversation in this direction, which he failed to do. Tell him(her) that while you would be glad to be with him in spiritual direction, there is something else. He clearly needs to do something about his general insecurity, and you do not feel qualified to assist him in this. Tell him the right professional assistance could prove very beneficial to him.

77. Isolation

Difficulties Presented: [middle-aged single woman] During her eight day directed retreat this woman told me that she was miserable. She was sure that God was asking her to open up to people and get close to them. Long since, she told me, she had built a wall around her so thick that nobody could get through and she was *content* to stay safely within. It was many years ago that she had solemnly promised herself she would never let herself get hurt again and she had lived that way. But during this retreat He had given her no rest whatever. She said, "I don't know if I could take down those walls. And I certainly don't know how I would go about it, if I did decide to try."

Underlying Meaning: In one way or other people realize that others can hurt them only if they let them. Only those they allow themselves to care about or to matter in their lives have that power. So, when some people are badly hurt by others, they protectively determine either consciously or below the level of awareness that they will put a stop to it. This they can readily do by turning off or tuning out all, especially positive, feelings for people. Needless to say this was not a well woman psychological-ly.

Suggestions On What To Do: You might reflect that any course of action whatever you might suggest could be extremely threatening to this woman. Here the Holy Spirit has taken the lead in *bothering* her within her safe psychological fortress. You might suggest to such a person that she(he) ask God what He wants her to do and how she is to go about it. In addition, you could remind her that God is most gentle. As she prays each day He will lead her to be open to Him and gently show her the steps to take in order to be the woman He wants her to be. Tell her you will add your prayers to hers. With this woman I was well aware that she could benefit from the right professional help. At the same time I sensed that by no means was such a referral or even such a suggestion during the retreat timely. I knew that I would have to wait and see if there would be such a time later on. I never encountered her again after the retreat. This person might get valuable help from a TRUSTED LISTENER (cf. Author's Foreword).

78. Jealousy and Envy

Difficulties Presented: [middle-aged married man] This man said that he found it most mortifying to have to admit to another person that he was jealous and envious of some other people. As he described his problem, he is so jealous of his wife that he is at times in torment when he finds her talking with another man. She is aware of this and it has almost been the cause for breaking up their marriage. He is also envious of other people, especially men, with whom he is continually comparing himself. He resents their superior education, larger car, better job, better looks, popularity, skills, etc. Any one of these can be a source of keen suffering for him at any given time. He is usually so angry that he cannot even go through the motions of praying.

Underlying Meaning: Occasional feelings of jealousy and/or envy are usually part of the human condition. Both seem to bespeak some insecurity. Both seem to result from the awareness that one is somehow threatened as a person. Jealousy tends toward destruction of the rival, as well. As occasional *feelings* both are not unhealthy psychologically, nor do they have any morality. The person who entertains or develops either one at least senses that doing so does not fit into a mature pattern of living. That is why it can be very embarrassing. Many a person has failed momentarily in fostering one or the other. Should such a cultivating be characteristic of someone, deep emotional problems should be suspected.

Suggestions On What To Do: You ought not be unduly concerned by one who acknowledges an occasional lapse in promoting either jealousy or envy. However if the admission were one of habitual failing in entertaining and fixating on either one, that is different. You are then dealing with an angry, insecure, and most likely, inadequate feeling person. In that case you would be wise to insist that your help with spiritual direction has a condition. That condition is that this person agree to also see someone professionally trained in dealing with the emotions for aid in that area.

79. Loneliness

Difficulties Presented: [middle-aged priest] It was during a retreat that this man said loneliness was the great cross in his life. He had found a woman in the parish with whom he could share his thoughts and this was a relief, but this sharing had developed into a physical relationship. This he said he had not planned on and really did not want, but it is there. He knows he can not afford to go near her. He added, "I thought I wanted my priesthood, and I still do, but I don't know. I can't take the loneliness."

Underlying Meaning: Was this *loneliness* or *aloneness*? It serves to point up the range of differences in the basic human social needs, for basic sociability. While it admits of degrees, every human has a need for someone else with whom to share what is important for him or her to share. The *healthy* range extends from those at one end who can live by themselves for long periods of time, miss the company of others, but take it right in stride. It ranges through those who, conscious of their strong need for relating to others, share an ongoing, warm, give-and-take relationship with certain other persons. Finally it approaches the other end where people are pretty much preoccupied with their social hungers, especially their need to be nourished by others.

Suggestions On What To Do: This man's needs might call for advising him to ask his bishop to place him where he would be within reasonable driving distance of two or three other priests. With them he might share, regularly and frequently, group activities such as praying together, playing poker, golf, tennis, bull sessions, etc. The bishop would be informed that this man *needs* this kind of companionship of other priests. Incidentally, a regular spiritual director can help fill this same need while helping him enrich his prayer life.

80. Love

Difficulties Presented: [older woman religious] After declaring that she wanted to keep the new commandment of Our Lord, this woman said there was one person whom she simply could not love. This person, her superior in religious life, had hurt her very deeply. She inquired, "How do you love a vicious phony?" She appeared hurt, discouraged and bitter.

Underlying Meaning: It is well to reflect here that a religious superior, as such, has the power to thrill or hurt many under her(his) authority in unique fashion. The devastating pain that such a person can cause in some people is indescribable. Hence, what might appear as overreacting in this nun could be her appropriate emotional response to the experience of feeling personally eviscerated. Even though this does not say a tremendous amount about the emotional stability of this woman, there need not be any need to suspect that the true explanation lies deeply hidden. At the same time her overall reaction does not appear to be a healthy one.

Suggestions On What To Do: A sensitive listening with compassion to a religious, particularly a woman, with this type of problem may free her(him) to begin to understand and cope with her hurt. Quietly pointing up the difference between the justifiable resentment for the *behavior,* while asking God's grace to be able to forgive the *person,* might help. It could also prove helpful to clarify that in order to love one who has proved untrustworthy, it is not required to trust that person. Rather, were the opportunity to present itself, hers would be the obligation of helping that person become trustworthy. Were you to sense the need for professional help for such a person it is highly unlikely you could bring it about. The problem needing attention she sees as that of the "vicious phony." In her view, her problem is that she has to find a way to put up with this person.

81. Love

Difficulties Presented: [middle-aged woman religious] It is a real conviction with this woman that she just can't let people love her. Why? "Because I get so much of it I just can't handle it." She has been a religious superior and knows that some of what looked like love was a counterfeit courting of her favor. The thought of this, incidentally, revolts her. As she looks back, she explained, she has had just too much love, affection, admiration, center stage, warm recognition. It is her wish that others who are hungry for love and acceptance would get some of it. She just can't absorb all the love she is receiving. So she has had to teach herself to accept it as something other than love. Accordingly warm expressions of friendship she sees as sympathy, fellowship, or something else. It had not occurred to her that when she viewed them as something other than love, they could not psychologically nourish her. During retreat she had an inkling that something was wrong with all this. Then she realized with a shock that she has not been letting Christ's love for her come in *as love*. She recognizes moreover that she is apprehensive about accepting His love for her as love. Now in utter astonishment she is beginning to become aware that she has never really let people love her, in fact she has not had much experience in accepting human love.

Underlying Meaning: This is an excellent example of one way the human psyche, operating protectively below the level of awareness, can completely fool a person. Here it is finding a justification for avoiding something the person was really afraid of, while remaining unaware both of that fear and of what was going on.

Suggestions On What To Do: As happened in this case, a person with this type of problem will recognize the nature of the problem when, and only when, she(he) is ready. This means she will see it when she is psychologically prepared to face and begin to cope with it, and presumably when God's grace is there, as well. Your most promising course with such a person is to continue patiently to listen to her. The presence of another listening, understanding, caring, non-judging person invariably seems to gradually free the one concerned to begin to deal effectively with her problem. In no way would I consider *clarifying* for her what is going on here. If she cannot afford to recognize it, such a 'clarification' could have a devastating impact. It could be felt as the violation of her person. If you could find a way, encouraging her to look for a TRUSTED LISTENER (cf. Author's Foreword) could pay rich dividends to her in accelerating her recovery process.

82. Love

Difficulties Presented: [middle-aged woman religious] During her retreat, this woman spoke of a large number of problems. She maintained that she could not feel love from others or other related emotions, and yet, in some cold, abstract way, knows God loves her. Yet she simply cannot trust Him completely. And she cannot relax. In her turn she feels no love for God and very little if any for people. Her fears are of what God might ask of her, what lies ahead, and having to face the unknown. She mentioned she has been hurt deeply by certain people, adding, "They fight dirty." Then she remarked, "I couldn't marry the man I was in love with, because I felt God wanted me to be a religious."

Underlying Meaning: This appears to be a non-free life commitment to religious life. As such, at some psychological level, it is experienced by her as a violation of self. She probably will not relate such painful feelings to the experience of being compelled to be in religious life. Moreover, this is in the context of a psychologically wounded person.

Suggestions On What To Do: At times you will find that a person has a deep, unshakable conviction that she(he) is not only not loved but also not lovable. No matter how indirectly she might put it, you know that she has been profoundly hurt in early life. Ultimately she is in need of professional help. Meanwhile, as you continue with her in spiritual direction, be alert. Do not let yourself begin to believe that if you can just help her clear up these problems, one at a time, she will then become a healthy, spiritually flourishing woman.

83. Love

Difficulties Presented: [young single woman] She declares openly that prayer is impossible for her, so starved is she for love. She lives to be loved. All the more so since she does not love herself. Socially she is most timid and shy. While she is told she looks peaceful, within she is filled with commotion, turbulence, and continuous anxiety. Depression is seldom absent. Her parents, she remarked, were both continually anxious and tense.

Underlying Meaning: My observation has been that parents who are chronically anxious and tense almost invariably have anxious and tense children. This type of inhibited woman may become an affection hunter. Her utter lack of self love, obsessive craving for love, and chronic anxiety, indicate a damaged personality. She might manage to latch on to a number of persons, one at a time, from whom she would derive some affection. If so, she would have no satisfaction of that hunger. She needs referral.

Suggestions On What To Do: Do not be completely surprised if you discover that she(he) hopes you will be the one to satisfy her hunger to be loved. It will not benefit her to tell her: (1) she will never satisfy this hunger, no matter how much affection she might receive; (2) it will never be enough nor of the right kind; (3) the void she is trying to fill has many of the characteristics of a child's longings and will prove insatiable. Gently as possible try to give her an early referral.

84. Loving

Difficulties Presented: [middle-aged, single woman] During the course of making a directed retreat, this woman said she cries whenever she talks of or even hears about loving others or about others loving her. She can't believe God loves her. Then she added, "My father married a woman from an ethnic group looked down on in our area. I was rejected even by my best girl friend when she found out about my mother. I didn't do anything wrong. They rejected not only me but my parents and all my brothers and sisters. I and my brothers and sisters really loved each other. Dad was cold and inhibited, so he couldn't show any of his love. I hated my mother, a wonderful, intelligent woman, because I felt that somehow she was to blame. I hated my father for what he did to my mother, especially on the score of his jealousy, and to one of my sisters whom he beat because she would not knuckle under."

Underlying Meaning: There is no question about the poignancy of her hurt. There does seem to me to be question about the totality of the rejection at its source. She seems to be saying that her father really loved, but was utterly unable to communicate that love. In its psychological impact that is very different from a lack of love. She later came to hate her mother, from the peer pressure. Never does she indicate that this wonderful, intelligent woman was not a loving mother. And there was love among the siblings. Accordingly, while such a woman might indeed be in need of professional treatment, substantial help from the right spiritual director is not, in my judgment, ruled out.

Suggestions On What To Do: Were you just to listen as such a person unburdens herself(himself) of all this, it could be very helpful. She might be able to work her way through this whole hurt in the presence of another listening, caring person. This is something that would be almost impossible by herself. The anticipation is that in order to have a chance to succeed in this, she would need a large number of spiritual conferences. On the assumption that she could manage this, there would be little you would have to tell her. As her hurts would lessen, her vision would begin to clear. After a good number of conferences, if you became convinced that your careful listening was not in any way freeing her, then you might consider referral. If she could find a TRUSTED LISTENER (cf. Author's Foreword), it could be very helpful to her.

85. Masturbation

Difficulties Presented: [middle-aged single man] During a directed retreat this man remarked that since he was a youngster he has had the problem of repeated masturbation. This baffled him precisely because he found himself repeatedly indulging a behavior which he really did not want. Even frequent confession did not seem to give any notable help. Since he has reached adulthood he has been aware that somehow fear is associated with this problem. He says openly that he does not understand it. Yet he feels certain that it has some tie-in with fear. He added, "I have a strong suspicion that when I begin to understand the tie-in with fear here, I'll be able to cope with this problem, and perhaps even help others who are wrestling with this problem."

Underlying Meaning: After he broke the ice and began to speak about his problem openly, the words just poured out.

He remarked that he had never before been able to talk openly about this whole area. As he spoke he noted aspects and meanings he had not even suspected. He observed clearly for the first time that he has been deathly afraid of sexuality. He had good reason to feel afraid for he was fearful that in any area of interpersonal sexual activity he would soon lose control. Then he recognized his masturbation as an immature 'payoff,' that is, a puerile way of saving him from having to face the fact that he had never dealt with his sexuality in a grown-up, total way. Instead he had intellectualized it. His basic conviction was that he had by no means completed his development in this area.

Suggestions On What To Do: Hopefully, no matter how clearly you saw the underlying meaning you would appreciate the inadvisability of suggesting any of it to him(her). Such a suggestion could be threatening to him. The psychological defenses he would automatically and unconsciously have to throw up against accepting this could seriously interfere with his spiritual and psychological unfolding. What, then, are you to do besides listen? You may need to remind yourself again that you are not *the* spiritual director of this person. The Holy Spirit is. You are here to give a hand when and if you see that one is called for. That is the point of your always saying a little prayer together ahead of time. The Holy Spirit will not only help this person but you, his spiritual director, as well. If there is something else you need to do, you will sense that. You might tell such an individual that were he to find a TRUSTED LISTENER (cf. Author's Foreword), much help could be found for him in this relationship.

86. Masturbation

Difficulties Presented: [middle-aged single man] I encountered this man in a directed retreat. He impressed me as a very good person. He was not free to marry in the Church. Almost from the beginning he pointed out that he felt he needed to talk about his sexuality. His frequent failing in masturbation left him feeling unspeakably low. Yet he did not seem to be able to get over it. He had prayed, fasted and done other penances to little avail. Just as soon as he felt lonely and unloved, he said, he would fail in this way again. At such times it invariably began with his fantasizing that some beautiful woman whom he had met somewhere would be taking him in her arms. As this fantasy continued he would invariably be aroused and then get no rest until he relieved himself.

Underlying Meaning: He saw readily, as he continued to converse, that the whole masturbation pattern was a means of getting something done; it was counterbalancing the feelings of loneliness and being unloved. Without his being aware of what was going on, his psyche had found a way of making up for or counteracting the pain with compensating pleasure. This connection he had not been aware of.

Suggestions On What To Do: Any focusing of attention on the masturbation itself would be to miss the purposiveness here. It would be to concentrate on the means being used without recognizing what was going on. It might be well to explain to him(her) that this whole operation of hurt and compensation are at the *feeling* level, but not *just* feeling. In the feelings of being unloved and lonely there are *cognitive* (knowing) elements. These feelings, in other words, also imply the knowledge that no one that counts is around who really cares about him. So we are not working solely with feelings. Thus there are some grounds for suggesting to this man that he regard these feelings of loneliness and being unloved as *cues* reminding him how much he needs Jesus Christ. You could explain to him that he needs to find other options to handle these frustrating, painful experiences. Whatever acceptable *options* he comes up with, he is not going to experience success without God's help. A TRUSTED LISTENER (cf. Author's Foreword) might prove helpful to this man.

87. Masturbation

Difficulties Presented: [young single man] During a retreat I was directing, this man began to talk about his problem with masturbation. He said that he really could not understand why he had ever established this habit. The one thing that he was aware of was that he got very tense at times and this seemed to give him relief so that he could relax enough to sleep. As he talked he said he was becoming aware that there was more than just a moral problem here, although he could not say what else that might be. The other thing that surprised and baffled him was that he sensed a deeply buried anger within him. He had no idea at what or whom it was directed. Nevertheless, he felt sure that there was some kind of connection between the anger and the masturbation. He didn't have even a clue what that connection might be. To have to own such a masturbatory pattern, he remarked, was painful because it made him feel rotten.

Underlying Meaning: A spiritual director might well pay close attention to this man's feeling that this is more than a moral problem, without knowing any more than that. Since I listened to him for only a few days I never did find out what else was operational here. Did the tension come from the anger? Might he not, in conscience, turn his anger loose on the person responsible instead of displacing it in onto himself? Such questions at times must remain unanswered. At any rate, doing compulsively what made him feel rotten was certainly a hurtful, destructive thing.

Suggestions On What To Do: It is incredible how much it can mean to many a person finally to find someone who will listen. A worthwhile reflection here is that God has made us social by our nature. When we get all wrapped up in an emotional involvement we do not manage well in thinking things out all by ourselves. But with God's grace we can think them through if there is someone there listening and trying to understand. If you keep these considerations in mind you will, as a spiritual director, be able to help many persons.

88. Masturbation

Presenting Problem: [younger woman religious] It was during an eight day directed retreat that this woman came to me. What had baffled her, she said, was that whenever she started to pray, in or out of retreat, she was flooded with temptations to masturbation. These temptations were so powerful that she usually yielded. At other times she had very little trouble of this nature.

Underlying Meaning: Because of this specific pattern of appearances of the problem I suspected strongly some unconscious motivation. As she talked, covering quite a range of topics, she happened to speak of a certain man whom she greatly admired and was very fond of. Then as though feeling that she needed to justify this relationship to me she added, "There's no problem, because even if he asked me to marry him I don't think I would." Then she talked about something else. She never put two and two together. It did not occur to her that she had just said she was still keeping her option to marry open. As yet she had not committed herself permanently to her celibate religious state of life. She had no inkling of what was going on below the level of her awareness. Psychologically she could not afford to get too close to God. At some psychological level she knew that this behavior was displeasing to God. Hence it kept her safely distant from God so that she could still hold on to her options—permanent religious life, or leave and marry.

Suggestions On What To Do: I did not feel that I should suggest anything during this short period. To have pointed to what I thought might be going on within her(him) could have been very menacing to her, giving her a sense of being trapped. In the case of a person with such a problem what should you tell her? After considerable prayer you would do well simply to do what you felt best under the circumstances.

89. Masturbation

Difficulties Presented: [middle-aged single woman] While I was directing this woman in an eight day retreat, she said, "When people tell me that God loves me, in a way I know this. And yet that means very little because I can't believe it or feel it. He couldn't. Look at my record. Look at the masturbation."

Underlying Meaning: She didn't get much beyond this in terms of indicating her difficulties. What was she manifesting? To begin with there were clear indications of a lack of self-acceptance. Her assumption that one must be worthy to be loved probably would not readily yield to correction. Why? Most likely she would need it to sustain her unacceptable pattern of masturbatory behavior. On what score? Because without any awareness on her part, something within her *needs* this pattern of unacceptable behavior. One possible explanation, of which she would not be conscious, would be that without this behavior she would have to admit that God does love her. If so, she would have to surrender to His love. This, I suspect, she would be deathly afraid to do. My sense is that she is certain that she must keep the controls over her life. There is a funny kind of logic here, but nevertheless a real logic which goes on below the conscious level, enabling the psyche to protect the person. Here is her logic of the example we have just used. If there is masturbation, then there is reason why God could not love her. But if He does not love her she has no need to surrender to His love, and so does not have to surrender the controls. Therefore, she needs the masturbation to hold off His love. Whatever the underlying meaning, she does not have any notion that there is one, let alone what it might be.

Suggestions On What To Do: Here I think it is more important to know what not to do. Your heart will go out to a person such as this, since she(he) is going through her own private hell. Your tendency will most likely be to help persuade this woman that God does love her. That can only threaten to strip her of her needed psychological defenses. It could become a desecration of her person. You should not emphasize the masturbation as the problem to be focused on. You both know its morality. You, however, also sense that it is saying something that at some psychological level needs saying, satisfying some hidden psychological need. If the right kind of professional help is available you might want to refer her. If she repeatedly comes back to the masturbation, you might simply listen and if pressed for a position inform her that because of the emotional factors involved you do not feel professionally qualified to evaluate adequately this behavior.

90. Masturbation

Difficulties Presented: [younger single woman] It took considerable courage and some time before this young woman whom

I was directing in a retreat was able to attempt really talking to me. As a young girl at home, she said, she was to be seen and not heard. Her mother dominated her completely, so that it was with a sense of escape from an intolerable situation that, at the end of high school, she left home. The invitation of a woman friend of the family made this possible. She was invited to come and do her best at a home for girls close to her age. Unfortunately, this friend took over where her mother had left off. She was not even to leave the house without permission. When she went out of the grounds she was to report back to this woman in detail what she had done. By experience she found that any idea or suggestion she had was neither welcomed nor needed. She was told what to do. In addition she was informed that this was all she needed to know. She was publicly corrected even for picking out 'wrong' articles in the supermarket. It came as a surprise to her to realize she had developed a rather constant practice of masturbation. Though she had confessed it, the pattern reappeared time and again. Fasting, bodily penance, and prayer, especially during Lent, had failed to help. She could not even think of leaving and going it on her own. She had no place to go. That was most frightening.

Underlying Meaning: This young woman was being suffocated as a person. She had no other options either for expressing herself or for experiencing pleasurable compensation for the frustration of being personally nullified. Any one of her classmates, in a frustrating situation might have compensated by going on a shopping spree, to a movie, etc. None of these was open to her. In addition, she was repeatedly being told, in effect, that she had nothing worthwhile to say. Little wonder that she lacked confidence in her own judgment and abilities to express herself in any significant way.

Suggestions On What To Do: Gradually you might feel your way in bringing such a person to see what her(his) problem really is. Having recognized it she could begin to search for smaller, safe, personally acceptable ways to manage self-expression and compensation. Then she would have to cope only with the pleasurable attraction of masturbation. Meanwhile if she could manage some counseling, she might be helped gradually to build her self-esteem and confidence. For years she had allowed herself to be kept, in some respects, as a child. Considerable time would be needed for her to correct these unhealthy growth patterns. A TRUSTED LISTENER (cf. Author's Foreword) could be helpful to her.

91. Masturbation

Difficulties Presented: [younger single woman] Since she was four or five years of age, this woman said, she had practiced masturbation on the sly because her mother had told her it was bad. The pattern persists and it bothers her because she is convinced that it is displeasing to God. This holds even though, she reports, more than one confessor has told her it is not wrong. She cannot explain to herself why this behavior should have continued and why she should not be able to terminate it once and for all.

Underlying Meaning: It is difficult to say what could be at the bottom of this pattern. Originally, most probably she experienced this as something pleasurable quite by accident and repeated it. After her mother discovered it and told her it was bad she continued it secretly. Why? An expression of her rebellion against her mother? And if so, what is it now? Still a manifestation of her unsuspected rebellion against adult authority? She has not even a suspicion that there is any underlying explanation, let alone that such might be the explanation. There is one consideration that might be helpful here. In my experience of spiritual direction I have noted that, when a woman has been awakened sexually to the experience of sexual pleasure well *before her puberty,* her sex drive remains persistent and strong throughout her life. I have not seen this noted by anyone else, so it well may not be correct. If it is correct, it would help explain why one who has been early awakened sexually and has no licit outlet for her sex drive would be sorely tempted and most likely in her previously learned pattern of experiencing sexual pleasure. The anticipation is that this temptation would be experienced distinctively in conjunction with her monthly cycle. If, in addition, she finds an unquestionably compulsive character to the tendency rather than one of simply yielding to a strong temptation, this may indicate one or more below conscious sources for these happenings.

Suggestions On What To Do: As you listen to such a person you might sense you ought to encourage her(him) not to give up the fight, for a good person can find such defeats very discouraging. This may be the time you say an extra prayer to the Holy Spirit, not knowing what else to do. You could well reflect that she will detect and benefit from the fact that you feel for her and do not think less of her in any way. There are no nice, neat methods for helping such a person with this problem. God's grace can do it. Tell her this, and offer to unite your prayers with hers that He will give her this grace.

92. Masturbation

Difficulties Presented: [younger single woman] During a retreat this young woman reported that for a few years she has had a pattern of fairly regular masturbation. As she spoke of it she mentioned the vivid imagery connected with it. She is invariably relating warmly and affectionately to a happily married man she knows, admires and is secretly in love with. She remarked that he would be utterly surprised to hear this. Frequently she relates affectionately to this man in fantasy and sometimes that is as far as it goes. At other times the affection moves into the passionate, and her hands stroking her own body, in most vivid imagination, become his.

Underlying Meaning: This is not really a masturbation problem. Rather because of the strikingly strong imagery involved this is an interpersonal problem which manifests itself sexually. She has not given up this man in the sense that she is still trying to keep him in her life in a way that is not licit.

Suggestions On What To Do: Given a person with such a problem, you will do well gently to call her(his) attention to the fact that this is not primarily a sexual problem. It is one of a relationship to another person which does not fit morally with the other's state of life. Even her 'masturbation' is perceived by her as an interpersonal happening. Accordingly, to place the stress on avoiding illicit sexual behaviors would be to focus in on symptoms at the cost of missing the underlying cause. Primarily, she is simply unable, in conscience, to reconcile this, her relationship, to the marriage vows of the man in her fantasy. Your personal support while she prays and works her way through such a problem may be of the utmost importance to her. It is well to tell such a person that by herself she is simply not going to have the strength, regardless of her generosity, to terminate this relationship without God's special grace. Tell her you will be with her in requesting that grace.

93. Mood Changes

Difficulties Presented: [young single woman] The first time this young woman came, though obviously pregnant, she manifested amazing energy. She talked rapidly and continuously. This she did while moving constantly about the room. Her conversation was most difficult to follow as she skipped and jumped from one topic to the next. Her mother told me that she had not been to bed for days. Yet she was tireless. Some weeks later she was brought to me by a member of the family. The picture had changed remarkably. She did not move from the chair nor even stir in it. Her speech, slow and weak, was marked by long pauses. What she finally did get out was a doleful remark that she did not see any point to living.

Underlying Meaning: Within a reasonable range we all have our up and down days. This was by no means within such a range. To me this had the appearance of manic-depressive psychosis (a serious mental illness of excessive emotional highs and lows). This illness can be brought into remission through proper medication, even though it tends to repeat periodically.

Suggestions On What To Do: If and when a person's mood swings are such that you sense clearly this is outside the normal range, try to talk not to the person but to that person's relatives or close friends. Tell them this person needs to see a psychiatrist who can prescribe the medication needed to help. It is wise tactfully to avoid the initiation of any spiritual direction at such a time.

94. Negative Feelings

Difficulties Presented: [later middle-aged, woman religious] It didn't take this woman long to make it clear that she has had an array of painful experiences. Prominent among these were fears, nightmares, nervousness. She was terrified of having to read in church or chapel. She said she had no interest in anything and emotionally was just flat. Yet to this was added depression. She has always been glad to pack and leave any house, no matter how many years she had spent there. The only roots she has are still in her childhood home. Only her brother and his children live there now. No matter. So often she reflects, and even did so at her final profession, "What's this charade all about?" She has never been able to say no to people because she couldn't dream of hurting them. "My family would have been most disappointed if I had left religious life. So I couldn't leave. And yet it's not my vocation. It's God's call, so I feel I am trapped." She remarked that death would be so welcome, such a relief.

Underlying Meaning: In addition to the vocation problem, the picture here is of one who appears never to have grown to full emotional and personal adulthood. It is the portrait of an adult female who experiences the helplessness of a fully dependent little girl when faced with a wholly adult problem.

Suggestions On What To Do: With such a one, perhaps you would do well to expect frustration (at times even an inclination to say, "Please try to act your age.") and the testing of your patience. One who is chronologically and physically an adult, while as yet a child within, does not have a child's refreshing, ingenuous, and redeeming qualities. What will perhaps particularly chagrin you will be her(his) utter inability to see that at least some of her own views, feelings and behaviors are unmistakably improper to an adult person. While many a little child can be a delight, this type of childish person never is. If you are willing to take her and not set your sights too high, fine. Still she will need accompanying professional assistance. At present I would judge that she does not possess the requisite maturity to make a serious discernment about her vocation.

95. Own Will

Difficulties Presented: [middle-aged priest] It was during an eight day retreat that this man came. On the basis of God's gifts to him and his God-given interests, he remarked, he has known for years that there is one specific kind of work God wants him to do. Now he is angry with God because he has met so much resistance in his every attempt to carry out this labor. Moreover, now his health is beginning to give way. "That is one hell of a way," he says, "for the God I have served so generously to be treating me." The injustice of it especially, he remarks, deeply depresses him.

Underlying Meaning: The anger could well be the evidence that this good, generous man is committed to doing his will for God. He seems to be at the controls, calling the plays of how he serves God, and as long as God leaves it that way all is well. But let God either interfere or permit interference with his generous endeavors and out comes the anger. Hence his behavior and experiences could be expressing something of which he is quite unaware, but which is a need of a more serious, deeper nature. For instance, he might need such recognized achievement to prove his personal adequacy, something that would appear so preposterous to his thinking that were it mentioned to him as a possibility he could only laugh.

Suggestions On What To Do: When you have listened to the point where you sense the one with this type of problem is satisfied that you understand his(her) problem, you might say something like the following. "The generosity which you have shown without any question is seen and valued by God. At the same time is it at least conceivable that God might want you to do something else? Would you be willing to ask Him?" If he agrees you might start him on a process of discernment to discover what

God would want him to do. If he strongly resists, then one of two explanations seems correct. Either it becomes clear that he does not understand why he could not even consider such a possibility, or the reasons he gives for refusing are, in your judgment, by no means either reasonable or convincing. In either case reference for professional help would be indicated, but exceedingly difficult, I think, to bring off.

96. Prayer

Difficulties Presented: [middle-aged married man] It was over the course of many months that this good man reported constant frustration with his prayer life. He was very faithful to his daily prayer, at a considerable sacrifice, since he was a very busy person. The frustration arose from the utter lack, during his prayer, of any consolation or joy whatever. He had at first reasoned that it must be his fault, but no matter how much he had examined himself he could find no grounds in his life for anything that would be displeasing to God.

Underlying Meaning: My impression was that this was a well-balanced, psychologically healthy man. In my experience God often appears to give consolation and joy, to a person faithful to prayer, early in life. This has been the experience, for example, of a large number of women and men religious. We often see a generous follower of Christ impatient to 'master' prayer. At times such persons react to dryness and distraction in their prayer with discouragement. They do not appreciate that this is what happens when God leaves a person to pray on his own. Neither do they really grasp that all consolation in prayer is GIFT from God. So when one of these says, "I don't get anything out of prayer," one wonders whose yardstick for successful prayer is being used? This person's or Christ's? And is this person's motive to get something out of it?

Suggestions On What To Do: Check whether he(she) understands and accepts it that consolation in prayer is not a human, learned achievement but rather God's gift. See that he is recollected beforehand and begins his prayer well. After that, if time drags, he wanders mentally, distractions abound, and sleep may even take over, what then? That can be a tortuous experience. Is it therefore an unsuccessful experience? According to whom? Did Christ say clearly that it was not a good prayer period? Is it not a successful period because it was without consolation and joy? Some succumb to the temptation to seek the consolations of God rather than the God of consolations. Explain to him that we don't know why God at times leaves us on our own in prayer. If, however, you sense clearly that this person *needs* consolation in prayer his psychological health comes into question. He may need psychological help as well.

97. Prayer

Difficulties Presented: [younger middle-aged, single man] This man reported experiencing constant, intense frustration in his prayer. He explained that he has tried everything he knows in addition to what anyone can tell him and still he cannot get anything out of prayer. Very serious about his spiritual life, it is of the greatest import to him that he do so. In fact, as a result of these painfully experienced frustrations, he described himself as a dam just waiting to burst. He added that he has no peace.

Underlying Meaning: Screened behind this man's problem lay high evaluations placed on prayer and on his relationship to God. Beneath all these I sensed one engaged in a hunt to satisfy compelling needs. He was not at the time open to letting God decide what he should receive from his prayers. Rather he felt he was being pushed to the breaking point by being denied from prayer what he felt he had to have. Increasingly he appeared to be a person who finds his self-concept quite unacceptable. Prayer was his avenue for getting the proof of his self-worth from his experience of God. Accordingly, to be denied such proof he found maddening.

Suggestions On What To Do: Gently endeavor to discern whether he is open to let God decide what he should get from prayer. You might mention to him one of the following points: Prayer is not primarily a means to satisfy a person's specific needs. God may not grant those of our requests that are bad for us. God does not reinforce our erroneous conceptions. Should you encounter resistance to such ideas you could be confronting one who is driven. A driven person does not feel free even to see, let alone follow out, any need to change his prayer attitudes. Such compulsive patterns will not be adequately ameliorated by spiritual direction alone. They call for a professional relationship as well. Normally if the right kind of professional help is simply not available, such attitudes might be slowly altered through a TRUSTED LISTENER (cf. Author's Foreword) relationship.

98. Pride

Difficulties Presented: [younger middle-aged, single woman] After a number of days of her retreat, this woman commented that she felt she was not making much progress. She knew why. It was her conviction that she was given to pride. She explained she has always relied solely on herself and so avoided depending on others as far as humanly possible. For instance she would never dream of asking another person a question which she could figure out or else look up. Now she sees her basic problem to be that of accepting her absolute dependence on Jesus Christ. It makes her nauseous to have to acknowledge her powerlessness to do anything whatever that merits her redemption. That in and of herself she can do absolutely nothing salvific appears to her almost impossible to concede.

Underlying Meaning: Here behind clear indications of intelligence, competence and overstressed self-reliance there appeared a lack of freedom and some insecurity. I sensed that she was not entirely a free woman.

Suggestions On What To Do: Inasmuch as I remained uncertain about the real sources of her difficulties, I would have no definite suggestion to make. However, listening at length to one with this pattern of difficulties you might be able to see what her(his) basic difficulty was. Would it look more like the need to prove herself or avoid the vulnerability of being dependent on someone else rather than pride? On the other hand, might she not gently be brought to recognize that complete dependence on Jesus Christ is not a weakness but a strength? Were she shown why, she might conceivably be able to handle things without professional help.

99. Psychological Protection

Difficulties Presented: [later middle-aged priest] When I was directing this man in a 30-day retreat, he reported that he prayed on scripture daily and came up with beneficial insights. His prayer, he explained, consisted of biblical explanations, based on the best of modern scholarship, archeology, critical analyses and commentaries. In short, he was talking about biblical exegesis. At no time was there any dialogue with or personal relating to the Triune God during these prayer periods. Impersonal, objective biblical criticism and interpretation constituted the entire content of his 'praying with scripture'.

Underlying Meaning: I never did clearly see what was below this pattern of 'praying'. It could be any of a number of things. After several days I gently mentioned the importance in prayer of relating to God, person to Person. He did not seem to hear it. Later when I again mentioned it, he bristled, became somewhat confused, and showed anxiety. So I backed off and permitted him to continue his pattern. I sensed that here was a very good man who seemingly could not psychologically afford feelings, at least toward the Persons of the Trinity. I noticed his characteristic standoffishness and aloofness in dealing with other persons, as well. This was unmistakable the few times the retreatants were permitted to relax with one another.

Suggestions On What To Do: I question whether this type of person could be referred for professional help. Regrettably, such psychological difficulties must restrict his(her) apostolic effectiveness. Your listening to him should do no harm. Neither would it be calculated significantly to benefit him. I do not think this type of person would be interested in having a spiritual director outside of retreat time.

100. Recognition

Difficulties Presented: [later middle-aged priest] From the first conference in his 8-day directed retreat this man continued to talk almost without a pause. He said he was utterly baffled by some of his behavior and in the worst way wanted to understand what was going on in his life. After a time, the foundation of his trouble became apparent to me. Yet he continued to talk all around it without clearly recognizing what it was. As I continued to listen I marvelled at how close he could come to seeing it and then go blindly right on by. I did not at any time show him what I saw at the root of his problems. Finally, near the end of the retreat he was almost bowled over with the discovery of what was long since clear to me. He was triumphant about his insight and most eager to apply it in his daily living.

Underlying Meaning: To begin with there was no indication here of serious pathology. Then, there was the strong, persistent urge in this man to talk continuously, practically without interruption. This is one of those situations where you trust that the Holy Spirit, at least thus far, is not asking your direct intervention in guiding this person.

Suggestions On What To Do: A general rule of thumb I try to follow is: Do not interrupt. When you would have to break in on him(her) in order to get a hearing, it is better not to. As long as he is most eager to continue talking it often means readiness for some spiritual (and frequently psychological) growth. The patience for this kind of restraint on your part, especially when you deem that what you have to say could be helpful, is achieved only with God's grace.

101. Rejection

Difficulties Presented: [younger middle-aged, single woman] From her earliest memories this woman recalls that she always felt the ache of knowing something was wrong but never knew what it was. Coming from a large Catholic family, she was assumed by others to have had a wonderful home life. Only recently has she been able, with the help of another understanding person, to face what in the pit of her stomach she somehow vaguely knew, but never could look at—her mother did not want her. She can never recall her mother expressing tenderness, affection or love for her. She always felt she was in her mother's way. She has often been told that during her first few months she got extremely sick to the point where they thought they were going to lose her. Her father, never her mother, often spoke of taking care of her during that illness. All she can remember of her mother's relating to her was the constant nagging, criticizing, and being made to feel she was no good. Her memory is of crying herself to sleep at night and, even when someone would reach out to her, she would shun that person because no one would ever understand. Now she feels like two people. One is the 'masked' one whom people see. This one is balanced, capable, organized, able to take care of herself. The other is a baby crying for tenderness, intimacy, understanding. The more mature person gets impatient with the immaturity of the other, wanting to push her back underneath somewhere. Now she realizes she has to get these two people together in order to really be herself. This most painful undertaking, at times, seems utterly impossible.

Underlying Meaning: It is easy to compassionate such a person, but I wonder to what extent one who has not gone through such experience can fully appreciate this most hurtful of human experiences. This is the product of rejection by one parent. (Note: For the psychological damage to occur it suffices just that it be *perceived* as rejection). John Steinbeck in his *East of Eden* (Bantam Books, p. 240), says with astounding insight, through the mouth of the Chinese, Lee, "The greatest terror a child can have is that he is not loved and rejection is the hell he fears. I think everyone in the world to a large or small extent has felt rejection, and with rejection comes anger, and with anger some kind of crime in revenge for the rejection, and with the crime guilt—and there is the story of mankind. ...One child, refused the love he craves, kicks the cat and hides his secret guilt; and another steals so that money will make him loved; and a third conquers the world—and always the guilt and revenge and more guilt... Therefore I think this old and terrible story (of Cain and Abel) is important because it is a chart of the soul—the secret, rejected, guilty soul." While all things are possible to God, the ordinary expectation is that even with professional help, some of the resulting wounds will remain through life. Only one who has been through such pain can empathize with another who is suffering in this way, and the sufferer seems to sense this. The rest of us only hope we can really sympathize.

Suggestions On What To Do: Barring a miracle of God's love, a referral, which must be done with the utmost delicacy, in my judgement, is a necessity. My sense is that a professional who has personally experienced rejection, if you happen to know one, might be the better referral, provided, of course, that the professional shares her(his) deepest religious values. And while she is getting this professional assistance you could continue to function as her spiritual director.

102. Resentment

Difficulties Presented: [young single woman] In the course of an 8-day directed retreat, this woman who appeared to be in her late twenties said almost immediately that she feels resentful of Jesus Christ, so stays safely distant from him. "Why? Maybe because he's a man. I feel resentful of men—of all men— for all the put-downs of my life. And I feel resentful toward the institutional Church, because it epitomizes the male put-down of women."

Underlying Meaning: Many women have suffered put-downs and been hurtfully debased by men, including men who appear, at least, to be their intellectual inferiors. In this case she seemed to have been cruelly demeaned by some man or men. I would suspect, however, there was more involved in her feelings than that. The generalization to all men is logically unwarranted. Hence, her head should correct any such feeling she might have toward Jesus Christ. As the Bard of Avon might put it, "Methinks the lady doth protest too vehemently." I did not know what was deeply at work in her psychologically. What was clear was that we were dealing with more than just a spiritual problem.

Suggestions On What To Do: Being a spiritual director of a resentful woman can be a very sensitive undertaking. This is particularly so if the former is a male and the latter is resentful towards males. If you are a male spiritual director for such a person, you would be conscious that you are being evaluated, to see whether you are an exception. Your challenge may be to be kind, gentle but not patronizing and not allow yourself to be manipulated. This person might benefit from the right professional help. As a man, I have found it exceedingly difficult delicately to suggest professional assistance to such a person. It can so readily be labeled further male abasing. If you are a woman and can find the right male spiritual director for her, it could be very helpful for you to try to refer her while inviting her to him to continue to come and see you for a little friendly visit from time to time.

103. Self-actualization

Difficulties Presented: [middle-aged single woman] When this woman came to me she remarked she badly needed spiritual direction. Her explanation was that she needed it mainly for self-growth, especially self-fulfillment, and self-expression in the Lord. She said she feels guilty that she has neglected her personal development so long. Now she is certain that God wants her to focus on self-knowledge and self-becoming. She knows that it is His will that she concentrate increasingly on knowing and developing in every way the person He has made. Her prayer, at least for the immediate foreseeable future, she added, must be the prayer of petition that God will give her the profound knowledge enabling her to become the person she is capable of becoming.

Underlying Meaning: While self-actualization is a good thing, this kind of preoccupation with self and with self-becoming is neither psychologically nor spiritually healthy. This preoccupation appeared to be close to obsessive with this woman. It was at base not a 'giving' orientation but a 'getting' one, the very antithesis of authentic love. Yet I felt that this woman viewed it as genuine self-love. There are indications here of immaturity and personal inadequacy.

Suggestions On What To Do: You will find a lengthy listening to a person with this overall interpretation of her(his) psychological needs exceedingly fatiguing. Indeed it can become exhausting. I know of no simple rule of thumb you can employ to test whether such behavior is seriously pathological. However, try as gently as possible to show her one thing. If she focuses on God and gives the primacy to taking care of Him and His, He will take care of her. Then observe her reaction. If she remains adamant in her position, you may conclude that she is beyond your help. If, however, she is able to hear what you say and begins to modify her thinking and behavior even slightly, the situation becomes hopeful that you will be able to be the instrument that helps her.

104. Self-Concept

Difficulties Presented: [middle-aged married man] In the course of an 8 day directed retreat this man said he has spent his life concealing his real self from all others including his wife. He maintained that he has had to play roles, and so to lie, name-drop, etc. "After all everybody plays roles," he added. For him, mere physical proximity, he remarked, usually is not dangerous. In the exceptional case where it has been he has needed to get the threatening person as soon as possible out into a crowd. There no psychological intimacy would be possible. More than anything else he wants acceptance for his real self but knows that this is impossible, and yet he can't help wanting it.

Underlying Meaning: Here a flawed self-regard is revealed. His unspoken conviction is that were anyone clearly to view his real self that person would have no choice but be forced to reject him because of what he saw. He feels that he is telling his spiritual director all this but, nevertheless, not letting him see his complete real self, either.

Suggestions On What To Do: This person's psychological state puts blocks on his(her) spiritual growth potential. He needs psychological help along with the spiritual direction in order to grow spiritually. The earliest possible referral, then, would be indicated. At the same time you reassure him you will continue in spiritual direction with him, while another endeavors to assist him with his self-regard.

105. Self-Concept

Difficulties Presented: [middle-aged single woman] Her most vivid memory, this woman observed, was being sent away to boarding school when she was in the first grade. She recalls experiencing, even that early, heavy guilt feelings regarding sexuality. She added, "You know how the nuns fill your head with guilt, etc." All through the years she has had a very poor self-esteem. Looking for the approval of others has been most important in her life. She has needed to have all people like her. If they did and praised her, it embarrassed her. "If they only knew me!" she would reflect. If they didn't like her she felt devastated. She remarked that she has been full of fears all her life. Yet her greatest fault, she pointed out, is her lack of trust and confidence in God. For years she has been asking Him to let her experience His love for her. In something of an abstract manner she believes it. She expressed great concern that she does not know how to pray. "Maybe it's because I'm trying to do it and won't let Him do it."

Underlying Meaning: I saw this woman during an eight day directed retreat. My impression was that her being sent away to school in first grade registered in her, at some knowing level, as her parents' rejection of her. The result was a completely undermined self-esteem. There could therefore be no self-acceptance. The hunger for acceptance from others, of course, did not decrease. Her inability to trust God her Father could have been anticipated.

Suggestions On What To Do: You could continue to work with this person in spiritual direction. At the earliest opportunity, most gently explain that you do not feel qualified to help her with these injured feelings of self-worth. While she continues to come to you for spiritual direction would she consider getting help with these feelings from one who is so qualified? A TRUSTED LISTENER (cf. Author's Foreword) might be able to help her.

106. Separateness

Difficulties Presented: [middle-aged woman religious] Over a period of many weeks this woman talked about her strong inclination to leave religious life a number of times because of the "SEPARATENESS." I endeavored to clarify what this term meant to her. I found that it meant primarily, "Not being able to talk to anyone about some things."

Underlying Meaning: I have had a number of married women say substantially the same thing. There are things some women have remarked they could say only to another woman. A few have said they would feel the same way if they could find one they felt they could trust. There are women who have asserted they needed to say some things to a very understanding man, just as there are men who remarked they preferred a woman spiritual director. I have encountered many more women than men who feel that they simply have to share certain most personal things with another person.

Suggestions On What To Do: As you listen you will find that many a woman (and some men) will come little by little to share almost everything with you, her spiritual director, even if you are a man. She will ultimately feel relieved and may express it as, "You know me completely, as no other person on earth knows me, and yet you are understanding and accepting of me." (This is not the same as accepting everything she(he) has done. In fact, she is not asking for such acceptance.) In my experience this role of acceptance of the person is one which spiritual directors frequently play though this was not their goal. And while you may not grasp the dynamics of what is transpiring you will come to realize that it is something that was really needed by this person. Finally you will reach the point where you are able to judge whether you need to help a person, such as this woman, through a process of discernment of her vocation.

107. Self-Sabotage

Difficulties Presented: [younger middle-aged, single man] For a long time this man said he had experienced frustration, particularly because so much of his own behavior bewildered him. Every time he has had an opportunity for advancing occupationally, he has inevitably fouled up and lost the promotion. When it looked to him as if he had the chance to marry a wonderful girl, he repeatedly fell on his face socially, in her presence, and embarrassed her as well as himself. That, he remarked, has been the story of his life, despite the fact that he has tried each time to do the right thing. As he put it, "I can't win for losing." In addition to all these catastrophies, he must fight almost constantly against a suicidal urge, though he has no reason to want to take his life. He said he is desperate for help.

Underlying Meaning: Psychologically this has all the earmarks of hostility being turned in on himself, yet wholly below the conscious level. The anger which gave birth to this hostility could have come, for instance, from his basic lack of self-importance. That is something that is maddening. What grounds has he for any kind of self-esteem? The strong inclination (hostility) to damage or destroy can safely be directed inwards, without fear of retaliation of any kind. This kind of displacement of hostility onto one's self is not uncommon. It all goes on, however, with the person concerned perfectly oblivious to the whole thing. He has no idea regarding the source of the hostility. In fact he is not clearly aware that there is any hostility. Meanwhile he continues to be baffled at a number of happenings in his life. Normally such a person will not start to see what is really happening in all these perplexing experiences, without professional help.

Suggestions On What To Do: You could explain to such a one that personal feelings and inclinations can be pretty perplexing things. Yet if someone can find the key to what is transpiring it all will make sense. Accordingly you think it might be a wise move to give someone trained in these areas a chance to help him (her) find that key. This, of course, can be done while you continue with him in spiritual direction. It is important to remind yourself that professional help is really needed here.

108. Speech

Difficulties Presented: [middle-aged priest] Perplexed and frustrated at a wholly unexpected reaction this man came in shaking his head. He explained that some women religious are upset on the score of misunderstanding the meaning of his words to them. He had spoken to them of a woman's, including a nun's, deep needs for affection and love. This had disturbed them because they interpreted this to mean that he was saying each of them needed a man. To me he said, "I don't think I'm a chauvinist. I certainly don't want to be one. I really care about these women. I was trying to give them something which I thought would be helpful to them. I just don't understand how they could have taken such meanings from my remarks."

Underlying Meaning: It's well to reflect that some women have been harshly treated by men, including painfully demeaned by them. Obviously no man has the right to talk down to any woman, nor to any man for that matter. There are two considerations of which a priest needs to be mindful in talking about certain personal things to a group of women. One is that he may encounter in a few of them an ultra-feminist attitude which does not welcome a man's telling women anything of a sensitive nature about women. If he is aware of this, he will not cease saying what he thinks he should say, but do so very considerately. The other consideration is that at the other end of the spectrum are some women who put a priest on a pedestal and regard as coming from God what he says to them. His obligation from being thus perceived is to qualify carefully whatever he says to them, especially if it be of a delicate nature. He simply reminds himself that certain people are still going to take as gospel truth whatever a priest says.

Suggestions On What To Do: You could well remind such a person of the two above considerations. Tell him that regarding some of those who are ultra-feminist, no matter how circumspect he is he had better face, ahead of time, that he will not always win. After he has tried, discouragement has no place. As for those who put a priest on a pedestal, urge him, when discussing personal things with women, to consider saying as clearly as he can also what he does *not* mean.

109. Sufferings

Difficulties Presented: [middle-aged woman religious] Though her mother died too early for her to remember, this woman stated she can recall nothing but personal coldness from her step-mother. She said she is angry because of Christ's sufferings. It is because of them that she can't get close to him or trust him. While she feels she really doesn't understand this, she is sure she cannot accept Christ's sufferings. She is very hurt, as well, by the brutal brush-offs from others she has experienced. While she does not remember all the hurts she has received, she insists she is unable to forgive the persons responsible. She readily acknowledges being very easily hurt. Now she finds that she just cannot sit still to pray or read, and she cannot just do nothing. She is much more comfortable standing while talking to someone.

Underlying Meaning: She was baffled for weeks in trying to explain to me the importance of sufferings in her experience. She was positive that they were of the greatest moment but for the life of her she could not say why. Then she saw that Christ's sufferings symbolized hers. These, her sufferings, were built up around her original rejection by her stepmother and subsequent rejections by others. As yet she has not recognized that she is blaming God for these rejections. Accordingly, she has not forgiven God for them. All she knows is that she simply cannot even think of going to God for help.

Suggestions On What To Do: Listen. At the earliest opportunity refer this type of person for professional help if the right help is available. Do not respond to her(him) in the matter of her sufferings. That could lead to entrapment of you, her spiritual director, which could be hurtful to her. If she should see that she is mad at God, show her how to go about forgiving God in her prayer. This type of person should have professional help while she is getting spiritual direction from you.

110. Suppression

Difficulties Presented: [younger middle-aged, single woman] During a directed retreat this woman came to me. She had asked for an older man as a spiritual director. Normally, she said, she felt crotchety during time of prayer. Usually aware of some anger, she was not reluctant to talk about it to some extent. At the same time she suspected that she did not really want to look too closely at her anger. There was something more going on within her, she felt, because of the tension she frequently experienced in her thighs.

Underlying Meaning: As she talked during the retreat she became aware that the tension in her thighs was from suppressed anger. The anger was there all right—she felt it—but she was bewildered, because she had no inkling about what or at whom she was angry. Later she thought she understood the reason for the suppression. It was her fear that were she to start to express her anger she might not be able to control it.

Suggestions On What To Do: As long as you sense that such a person is making some headway in just talking you are reasonably safe in letting her(him) continue. It is even possible, though I don't think probable, that all she would need in order to work her way entirely through this problem would be an understanding, sympathetic listener. Were she to come to an uncomfortable halt in her apparent progress in handling her difficulties, what would you do? Tell her that a professionally trained person could help her understand why and at whom she is angry. These two areas could go hand in hand. While you would be seeing her for her spiritual advancement, this other person would be helping her with her psychological difficulty. The spiritual and psychological aspects of a person are very closely interrelated.

111. Surrender

Difficulties Presented: [younger middle-aged, single woman] When this young woman came for her retreat she was restless. Shortly before she came, she stated, she had begun to see that she was not letting God run her life. In fact, she knew she was still holding on to the controls. Her childhood and youth, she said, were hard and she had had to stand on her own two feet and be strong. Early in life she had learned that she was not to trust others, but rather be self-reliant. Now she wanted to do something about letting go but was afraid and didn't even know how to start.

Underlying Meaning: After a time it became clear to me that she was presenting a very accurate picture of her present problem and accounting correctly for its development. There was nothing undeniably pathological in this picture. The prospect of unconditional surrender to God is utterly terrifying to some very good people. This holds true particularly of those who have learned not to trust others. This was the picture in her case.

Suggestions On What To Do: At times you will sense that this is an expected outcome in view of a person's whole early interpersonal history. You might wisely tell such a one that since you are not sure of the best way to proceed, you suggest that she ask Our Lord what He wants her to do. This approach I often find advisable and use frequently in spiritual direction. This woman asked repeatedly and nothing came. One day she arrived in high spirits, walking two inches off the ground. Our Lord had answered her. She had discovered it in Philippians 2:6-7. "Make your own the mind of Christ Jesus:

> Who, being in the form of God,
> did not count equality with God
> something to be grasped.

But he emptied himself,
taking the form of a slave,
becoming as human beings are . . ."

With this as her model she began to surrender the controls of her life to God. I have often advised one who is asking God for an answer occasionally just to open up the scripture anywhere and begin to read. God is still communicating to each of us through the sacred scriptures, and this, as it were, offers God another channel through which to answer petitions. A person with this type of difficulty might benefit from a TRUSTED LISTENER (cf. Author's Foreword).

112. Tardiness

Difficulties Presented: [middle-aged single man] This was a prayerful, intelligent seminarian approaching ordination to the priesthood who was faced with almost insurmountable obstacles. These took the form, principally, of an inability to get academic assignments in on time. No matter what he tried he was not able to force himself to get a term paper, etc., turned in at the assigned time. Hence he was continuously asking faculty members for an extension on time for each assignment, without exception. He remarked that he also had real difficulty, on a number of scores, in seeing himself in the role of a priest.

Underlying Meaning: This could be nothing more than a persisting trait of his personality and character learned in early life, which people characterize as, "That's just the way he is." On the other hand it could be that something deeply within him is struggling to avoid priesthood, or is not yet ready for it. So while, in effect, dragging his feet, he would remain unaware of what is actually going on within him.

Suggestions On What To Do: You might assume, as a working hypothesis that the first explanation that this is just the way he is, may be correct. Accordingly in the course of the direction you would give such encouragement, reassurance and support as would seem suitable. All the while you would be listening for any indications of grounds for the second hypothesis that he is fighting his priesthood. Among these latter would be such things as expressions of doubts that he should be a priest, the experiencing of notable tenseness or some other physiological reaction associated with his thinking of future priesthood. Look, as well, for other signs such as increasing discomfort somehow related to his becoming a priest. Clear signs of the likelihood of the correctness of the second hypothesis could indicate a need for professional help, or help in vocation discernment.

113. Temptations

Difficulties Presented: [middle-aged married woman] She said that the evil spirit floods her with temptations. He has, she explained, kept her marriage on the rocks for years. He has forced her to say and do things which she would never think of doing. Now she has met a man who is kind, considerate and attractive. She is afraid she is going to have an affair with him. The temptations, she says, from the evil spirit to do so, are strong and persistent. She knows that ultimately she will be forced by the evil spirit into such a relationship.

Underlying Meaning: Attributing temptations and failings to the evil spirit may unwittingly be a way of displacing responsibility from self to another. This could be evidence of a delusion (an erroneous judgment that persists in the face of contradictory evidence) and so an indication of mental illness. At any rate while temptation is readily understandable, the conception of being *forced* by the evil spirit into an affair, etc., does strain credulity, to say the least.

Suggestions On What To Do: You cannot function as a spiritual director for people who are not responsible for their actions. You would be ill advised to try, by yourself, to help this woman as she is. Remind her that self-deception is always a possibility this side of the grave. Tell her that while she continues to come to you, you would like her also to get a second opinion from a good Catholic psychologist or psychiatrist about her being coerced by the evil spirit. This professional person would understand the psychological as well as the spiritual aspects of her problem. You can almost anticipate a refusal at even the mention of a clinician. Nevertheless, gently but firmly stick to your position. If she refuses, inform her calmly that you would be too uncomfortable to continue without the professional judgment.

114. Tenseness

Difficulties Presented: [middle-aged married woman] During her retreat this woman said that among many of her acquaintances she is known as a jolly, happy-go-lucky person. And this doesn't surprise her because she can and does put up a very good front. They don't even suspect that she is constantly tense with a knot the size of a grapefruit in the pit of her stomach. She explains that she can laugh off the remarks, the criticisms and the rumors for a while. What she keeps asking herself is, "Will I explode?" She added that she has come to the conclusion she needs a spiritual director for one purpose, namely to find out how to handle 'people hurts.'

Underlying Meaning: When this woman repeated remarks that had been made to her in pretended kidding, it became clear that some of them indeed could be deeply hurtful. At the same time, I asked myself, "Was she selectively hearing only the negative? Was she overreacting to remarks? Was she paranoid (seeing persecution by others where it existed only in her own mind)?" If a spiritual director strongly suspected that it was the last mentioned, she would clearly need referral for professional care.

Suggestions On What To Do: As you listen to such a person you may begin to get some clarification why she(he) is willing to take these hurtful remarks. Is she so terribly vulnerable that she has to be 'Mrs. Nice Guy'? Does she desperately need to be liked by everyone, so that people have learned she will take anything they say? Is there something about her that invites such remarks from others? If you should get some inkling of what seems to be at the bottom of this you might listen for her to bring it up so that together you could look at it. The one thing you would hold to is that this kind of tenseness is not healthy psychologically or spiritually. You may need to remind yourself that when you have no idea what to say, continuing to listen is wise. This woman might benefit by finding a TRUSTED LISTENER (cf. Author's Foreword).

115. Trust

Difficulties Presented: [middle-aged woman religious] She had told me earlier that her father had treated her very badly. Then she wrote, "After I left you I cried until early in the morning. I think I told you that at Mass, Tuesday, after communion, I told Jesus (from my stomach) that I trust Him. But Wednesday, when I awoke, there were words in my stomach, 'Jesus is to be trusted.' Not 'You can trust me' or 'Trust Jesus'. It was like I had a choice but I already had decided. In my meditation last night,

Jesus (and I knew He would) wanted to take me to that half-dream I had about Dad. I didn't want to. But it seemed okay if He were there. He embraced my dad and said maybe I'd want to, too. (It seemed that to accept him (Dad) there and embrace him would be to forgive him.) So I did. And then he was changed—almost like healed. But it was all a continuation of the peace I felt all day. I felt like that peace was like a butterfly in my hand and I was scared it would fly away any time. But, on the other hand, I knew, in my stomach, that even if it goes, 'Jesus is to be trusted.' "

Underlying Meaning: Of course, you would wisely listen to people, especially those who have been deeply hurt in interpersonal relations, talking of what they have 'heard' and/or 'seen' with considerable wariness. Yet every once in a while, in my experience, Jesus Christ (or the Father or Holy Spirit) touches someone as clearly as He did this woman whose 'hearing' I came to regard as authentic. I have rarely encountered this. When this does happen I would expect the person to carry some of the scars of the parental rejection, but the healing is amazing and the scars can be coped with. This type of healing is deep and lasting in a way psychotherapists would seriously hesitate to hope ever to achieve. The authentic nature of it is reinforced in that it remains for years.

Suggestions On What To Do: When you encounter someone in spiritual direction who reports some such experience, proceed very cautiously in evaluating it. If, as far as you can see, you judge such experiences authentic, just remind yourself that you are there to give that person an assist, if and when an assist is needed. Often a shared prayer of thanksgiving seems timely, as God appears clearly to be taking care of this person. Otherwise prayerfully listen. If, on the other hand, you increasingly question in your own mind the genuine nature of what she is reporting, then what? Tell her you are not comfortable continuing as her spiritual director unless she gets a second opinion on the dependability of what she 'hears.' Add that you would be at peace with such an opinion only from a professional person who is also a practicing Catholic, and whatever his opinion, you would like to be able to talk with him after she had seen him.

116. Turbulence

Difficulties Presented: [young priest]   About half way through his directed eight day retreat this man said that for some reason he had very little peace. He added, "I know that a person should be more rested and relaxed at the end of the retreat, but this turbulence is not diminishing." Asked if he had any notion what was the source of the disturbance, he answered, "Not really. It's funny but I sense somehow this is from God. I have the feeling that He wants me to do something, or perhaps to stop doing something. I'm afraid."

Underlying Meaning: A spiritual director has been given a clue in this pattern of experience to listen for an underlying meaning. This could be an indication from God. It could also be a temptation from the enemy. That meaning is presently hidden from him, and there is no one else who can help him see what it is. The anticipation is that as he is permitted to talk on, he will come to recognize what it is.

Suggestions On What To Do: You might suggest to one with this pattern to go to God in prayer just as he(she) is, afraid and perplexed, and ask for the grace to be open to what God wants from him. Then you could encourage him to ask God for enlightenment on this and also for whatever strength he would need. When he reports back to you, along with your spiritual discernment listen for anything that might seem unhealthy. A lack of peace can be an indication of psychological as well as spiritual problems, and yet need not be.

117. 'Visions'

Difficulties Presented: [middle-aged married woman] Only after considerable time in spiritual direction did this woman begin to tell me about the things she 'saw'. She felt she needed spiritual direction in these experiences in which she knew she could easily be deceived. Her 'seeing' was clear, detailed, and almost always in color. It had nothing of the hallucinatory about it (she was never completely unaware of the actual background of what she was 'seeing'). The experience I had was that her experience was analogous to that of a person watching T.V. in a dimly lit room. The person would be aware of the wall and other things behind the T.V., but not attending to any of these. Her 'visions' had the lucidity, detail, color and movement of T.V. She could experience them anywhere, at any time, with or without other people present. Color was very significant and meaningful. For instance, Jesus Christ had a particular color. So did the Father and the Holy Spirit. The evil spirit had both a distinctive color and a specific, revolting, insect shape. In at least some of these 'visions' God appeared to be communicating with her, showing her what in her life was pleasing and displeasing to the Father.

Underlying Meaning: When hearing someone talk of 'visions' my initial reaction is to be wary if not skeptical. In the great majority of cases I think that first reaction has been proven justified. In the present case, as the months passed, I became increasingly aware that this woman was not highly suggestive, given to flighty imagination, nor hallucinating. Rather she was open to direction, psychologically healthy and well-balanced and trying to live for God the way He wants her to. As I see it, God has been using her visual gift to communicate with her. Even though this woman does not go about talking about these 'visions', and so could not be identified by what I would say here, I do not feel justified in divulging some specifics of her 'visions' which could give you a much better basis for evaluating their authenticity.

Suggestions On What To Do: Once you hear 'visions,' tend to be leery of what you are going to be told. Usually when you pay no further heed to these reported 'experiences' the person concerned moves on to other things. If you are doubtful about the genuineness of her(his) 'experiences,' the Ignatian Rules for the Discernment of Spirits should be valuable. If you finally judge them to be gifts from God, pray for His ongoing grace to be open to understand the 'visions' if and when He wants you to.

118. Vocation Crisis

Difficulties Presented: [younger middle-aged, woman religious] For some time she has wrestled with her vocation. She said she has lived in crisis. Following the advice of her confessor, she wrote out all the reasons for staying and all those for leaving. Even after she did so, she found it terribly complex and confusing. "It still tortures me," she said. She wants to know what to do about her vocation.

Underlying Meaning: It would be perilous to generalize since such a problem could stem from any one of a number of factors. My hunch is that this woman is truthful in saying she does not know with certainty what God wants her to do, and she does not feel morally free in trying to resolve her problem. At the same time it is important to recognize the possibility that at some psychological level she may know to what God is calling her and yet afraid she would be personally violated in trying to follow it. This woman does not come across as a manifestly mature adult. Neither does she show a great deal of self-reliance, self-confidence or initiative.

Suggestions On What To Do: You might gradually help such a person see with certainty that she(he) wants to lead her life for God, so that is not in question. Her question is: *IN WHAT STATE OF LIFE?* You might then by degrees try to show her that she is really wholly free in God's eyes to choose her state of life. While there may be much that you do not feel you understand, you know that God does not want a slavish service in which one feels enslaved and violated as a person. You might try taking this person through a process of discernment. It is likely that the best she can do is not seek directly what God wants her to do, but rather what she wants to do for God.

119. Weight Problems

Difficulties Presented: [early middle-aged, married man] The first glance showed this man to be exceedingly heavy. He remarked that he had suffered most of his life from excess weight. Numberless times he has been deeply hurt by looks of disgust on the faces of slender people who run their eyes over him from head to foot. He has tried to laugh off the would-be kidding remarks about his size. Repeatedly he reminds himself that people do not realize how much they are hurting him. If they had any idea, the hurts would disappear. That, at least, is what he tells himself. Yet he only half believes it. He is terribly vulnerable, exposed to the whole world, and he receives little mercy from that world. Even his own children, by their looks, wound him.

Underlying Meaning: Many people do not appreciate that there are a good number of heavy people who cannot eat an ordinary amount at meals without putting on weight. Their weight is the cross of their life. They could hate thin people who can, and often do, eat anything they want without gaining a pound. The food these inclined to corpulence must rigidly confine themselves to, just to maintain their weight, appears more suited to rabbits than humans. Little wonder that some of them seem at times to give up and eat almost everything in sight with predictably disastrous results. There are very heavy persons who are compulsive eaters. That normally indicates an emotional problem. For instance, a very portly person can beat them to the punch. He may sense, below the level of his awareness, that people are not going to accept him because sooner or later they will see that he's really not lovable. So he selects the grounds for their rejection. He arranges it so that they will reject him because he is fat. This is much less hurtful than being rejected because you are clearly seen to be a nobody. In a word, inordinate weight can be a sign of psychological problems though it may be nothing of the kind.

Suggestions On What To Do: A notably obese person coming to you for spiritual direction might not mention the weight problem for a considerable time, if at all. If and when he(she) does mention it, you might receive an opening to ask if he is on a diet. If not, would he enlighten you as to why? The answer to this question might present you with the opportunity of suggesting a referral to a professional person while you continue with him in spiritual direction.